A Guide to College Resou
Financial Management

G000165991

Managing Colleges Effectively Series

General Editor: Desmond Keohane

A Guide to College Resource and Financial Management

Bob Lawrence

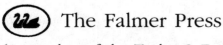 The Falmer Press

(A member of the Taylor & Francis Group)

London • Washington, D.C.

UK   The Falmer Press, 4 John Street, London WC1N 2ET
USA   The Falmer Press, Taylor & Francis Inc., 1900 Frost Road, Suite 101,
            Bristol, PA 19007

First published in 1995

A catalogue record for this book is available from the British Library

Library of Congress Cataloging-in-Publication Data are available on request

ISBN 0 7507 0445 4 cased
ISBN 0 7507 0446 2 paper

Jacket design by Caroline Archer

Typeset in 11/13 pt Garamond by
Graphicraft Typesetters Ltd., Hong Kong.

Printed in Great Britain by Burgess Science Press, Basingstoke on paper which has a specified pH value on final paper manufacture of not less than 7.5 and is therefore 'acid free'.

Contents

List of Figures

Acknowledgments

As is usually the case with the production of a book such as this, acknowledgments of help are due to many. Of these I have the space to name only a few:

- the members of the Editorial Board for the series of guides who have thoroughly reviewed the manuscript and made suggestions which have resulted in marked improvements, they are:

  - Desmond Keohane   Education and Training Consultant
  - Graham Wharton   Principal, North Oxfordshire College
  - Alan Wells   Deputy Principal, Reading College
  - Richard Evans   Principal, Cricklade College, Andover

- Noel Otley   Vice Principal (Curriculum and Quality), Oxford College
- Phil Garner   Head of Department of Student Services, Oxford College
- Richard Gorringe   Director, Norton Radstock College, Bath

to all of these, and the many others, go my sincere thanks. In particular I wish to acknowledge the use of information drawn from the many excellent publications available from the Further Education Funding Council some of which are listed in the Bibliography on page 197.

Introduction

This guide provides a practical resource to support the development of effective resource and financial management in colleges. It is designed to help governors and non-financial staff in colleges with financial responsibilities or those that wish to know more about college finance and want a practical guide that is easy to read, understand and use.

Users of this guide will find many of their questions on college financial and resource matters answered. They will be able to reinforce their knowledge through considering and completing the exercises at the end of each section and will also be able to supplement the information given with local materials and information about their own college.

Tutor support from the College Accountant or Finance Director will be necessary to provide:

- supplementary information (particularly in relation to some of the illustrations given and to provide definitions/explanations of key terms);
- guidance on how to complete the exercises together with feedback and model answers. This will need to reflect on the effects of location, type of college, for example, Sixth Form, etc.

As a result of working through the guide and completing the exercises we believe you will be able to understand:

1 How strategic and operational planning takes place at college level and how:

- the Business Plan is prepared;
- the Plan translates strategic and operational objectives, into concrete goals expressed in terms which are capable of quantification, achievement, being monitored and evaluated and costed within a specific timescale;
- financial risk is assessed;
- estates objectives are determined and costed.

2 How financial planning, management and control systems operate and how:

- financial management and control systems protect the college's finances and minimize financial risk;
- the college's financial objectives are established;
- your college's financial regulations and procedures are used;
- the concept of depreciation is implemented/used;
- the messages from the year end report and accounts are communicated;
- cashflow is managed;
- the system for staff monitoring and control operates;
- the information requirements for financial planning are established.

3 How business functions and services operate and how:

- effective control of purchasing can be achieved;
- the payroll service should be managed;
- effective treasury management can be achieved;
- capital can be raised and how to prepare a capital investment proposal;
- assets management is achieved, depreciation is treated and a replacement policy implemented;
- the college can plan for audit;
- the cost of contracted-in business services may be controlled.

4 How income and expenditure occurs and how:

- trends in income may be monitored;
- trends in expenditure may be monitored;
- income/expenditure variances from budget may be investigated;
- the funding methodology is used to establish your college's recurrent grant;
- the recurrent funding allocation can be analyzed by entry/on programme/achievement and by academic department.

5 Internal resourcing, unit costing and budgeting operates and how:

- outputs may be quantified through unit costing;
- resources are allocated in the college through the budgeting process and how financial forecasts are prepared;
- income and expenditure may be located at departmental level;
- staffing expenditure should be budgeted.

6 How performance measurement and monitoring operates and how:

- to establish and get the best use from performance indicators;
- actual performance is compared with budgets through budgetary control procedures;
- monitoring responsibilities are determined;
- targets are set;
- the information requirements for monitoring are established;
- FEFC performance indicator trends can be used.

7 How to improve efficiency and increase income and how:

- measures can be taken to improve efficiency;
- bottom line income can be increased.

8 How to make inter-college comparisons:

- and particularly how to compare your college with other similar colleges.

The Planning Framework

1.1 Introduction to the Stages of the Planning Process

A fully integrated business planning process enables dynamic strategic and operational planning in the college and ensures the level of central co-ordination required (see figure 1). The college's 'Mission Statement' provides the base from which to plan; sets out a clear view of purpose; identifies the college's values and distinctive features and provides the rationale for the strategic plan. In summary the stages of the planning process are as follows.

1.1.1 Stage 1 — The Strategic Analysis

The college's strategic and operational planning process begins with the production of the strategic analysis. It has three parts:

Part A is the detailed assumptions on which the planning process is based including an assessment of the effects on plans of variations in external factors, the likely consequences should these assumptions not be realised, and the actions which the college will take in such circumstances.

This is essential information for 'risk management', particularly financial risk management.

Part B is an analysis of market needs.
   This part of the strategic analysis informs the process by which level of activity and volume of work are estimated. Information is considered under the following headings:

- the customers;
- national labour market and skill trends;
- the strategy for skills and enterprise;
- the national employment situation;

Figure 1: The business plan

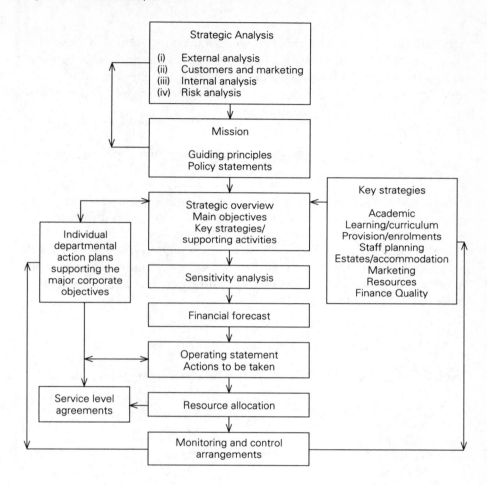

- the local situation;
- employers' survey data;
- local economic and labour market report;
- trends in the size of the market for education and training: Strategic implications;
- provision for those with learning difficulties and/or disabilities;
- plans for collaborative arrangements with external institutions, higher education institutions and schools.

Part C is an internal analysis of the college including consideration of strengths, weaknesses, opportunities and threats (SWOT).

1.1.2   Stage 2 — Review of the College's Mission, Guiding Principles, Policies and Strategic Directions

Each year governors and the college community should review the college's mission against changes that have been identified through the strategic analysis. This review will ensure that the strategic directions are still relevant. The strategic directions indicate the overall directions for the college over the planning period.

1.1.3   Stage 3 — Determination of Strategic Options and Objectives

At this stage a number of options are considered, subjected to an initial sensitivity and cost benefit analysis, priorities established and strategic choices made. The objectives on which the college will focus in support of the achievement of each strategic direction are stated as are the specific outcomes which will be used to measure achievement. Timescales are determined and expenditure necessary to achieve the objectives estimated.

1.1.4   Stage 4 — Review of Key Strategies

At this stage the college will review its key strategies which include:

- academic/curriculum;
- enrolment;
- marketing;
- estates;
- staff planning;
- resources;
- finance;
- quality.

All strategies should clearly support the achievement of the college's mission and strategic objectives. One of the most important strategies is the academic or curriculum strategy which is based on a real understanding of the needs of the college's customers and the community. The academic strategy will form the basis for:

(i)   a clear definition of current and future programmes including:
- continuing provision;
- revised provision;

- new provision;
- discontinued provision;

(ii) planned levels of student recruitment per programme area together with the associated planned funding unit levels;

(iii) planned outcomes/achievements for all students;

(iv) identification of funding consequences — income/expenditure.

1.1.5   Stage 5 — Production of the Annual Operation Plan

The annual operation plan, which flows from the above, shows how during the next year the college will achieve its specific objectives, in what timescale and who is responsible for achieving these. It specifies the many tasks that will need to be undertaken and how they will be resourced.

The annual operating plan represents the tactical execution of college strategy. Its financial expression is in the form of a master budget which provides an aggregate view of the college's operating plans and budgets and which comprises:

- a profiled (month by month) college budgeted income and expenditure account for the year;
- a projected balance sheet as at the end of the year;
- a month on month cash budget for the year.

Data contained in the academic plans produced by each department (see figure 2) provide the basis of the college operating budget. Support centre budgets may be apportioned to departments and form part of their budgets. The basis of apportionment will depend on the factors influencing the level of expenditure. (for example, premises expenditure is influenced by number of rooms/space allocation, whereas student services expenditure is influenced by numbers of students).

The use of priority-based budget reviews involving presentation and justification of the content of each development plan should prevent automatic year-on-year incremental increases without considering:

- the continuing need for the activity and its relative priority;
- the required level of service;
- efficiency and effectiveness;
- alternative approaches, ie the learning process.

Figure 2:   *Departmental action plans*

The diagram illustrates how individual curriculum action plans support the achievement of the major college objectives within the framework of key strategies, for example, academic, finance, quality, etc.

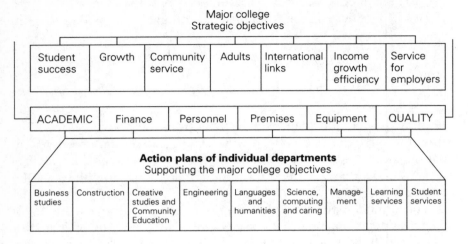

1.1.6   Stage 6 — Allocation of Resources

Resources will be allocated to carry out the tasks under each specific operational objective. Service level agreements are also prepared in liaison with budget managers and these link the budgets with the level of activity and the achievement of each objective (an example of a service level agreement can be found at section 5.5). These service level agreements also help to ensure consistency in the operation of quality assurance procedures.

1.1.7   Stage 7 — Ensuring Quality

The whole process is underpinned by a quality assurance system including a college quality policy and plan which is used as the basis for the continuing review and evaluation of quality. It is essential that management information requirements at different levels within the college are clearly established and agreed as part of the process.

In summary for Further Education purposes the business plan is:

The translation of strategic goals into concrete objectives, expressed in terms which are capable of:

- quantification;
- achievement within a specific timescale;
- being monitored;
- being costed;
- and eventually being judged as effective or otherwise.

The business plan is an 'action plan' which converts the rather general objectives of strategy into specific attainable goals and identifies the steps necessary to achieve them and what finance and resources are required.

1.2   Financial Management and Control Systems

The college's resourcing policy operates within the framework of management controls and procedures. The main documents which provide this framework include the Financial Memorandum and the college's Financial Regulations and Procedures. Financial management and control systems and procedures, covered in Section Two of this guide, are necessary to maintain adequate control of financial affairs and protect the college from financial risk.

1.3   Financial Memorandum

The financial memorandum sets out conditions for the payment of the funds by the FEFC to the college, including accounting and auditing procedures. It is in two parts:

- terms and conditions applying to all colleges;
- an annual funding agreement between the Council and the college which links the volume of activity to the amount of funds allocated.

The main points from the memorandum which provide the financial framework in which the college must work include:

- details relating to allocation of recurrent and capital funds;
- virement rules;
- payment of funds — how and when;
- land and buildings — any change proposed must have prior approval from the Funding Council;

- rules relating to borrowing;
- requirements relating to audited year end accounts;
- audit requirements.

1.4   Internal Resourcing

Colleges are not profit seeking organisations but aim to provide a balanced portfolio of educational provision and learning support for students. This requires resource provision for courses to be at levels which are sufficient to, at least, break even when delivered at acceptable levels of quality and productivity.

1.5   The College's Resourcing Policy

The college's resourcing policy should be driven by the college mission and curriculum and not the reverse. The activities and the tasks which it has been agreed should be undertaken by the college to achieve the objectives must generate the resource not the other way round. Developing a resourcing model which reflects curriculum priorities is likely to involve:

(i)   the analysis and comparison of unit costs of programme areas and services (see section Five);

(ii)   reviewing allocation mechanisms to encourage growth of underrepresented groups and to 'protect' a balanced curriculum offer in the college. (This will often mean that applying an internal resource allocation formula on its own will not be appropriate and resource allocation through the more subjective planning process will be the most suitable for colleges to maintain a balanced curriculum.);

(iii)   establishing a costing methodology and pricing policy for College services (see Section Four);

(iv)   determination of performance indicators in order to demonstrate that central services, funded by internal top-slicing, are operating as cost effectively as other areas of provision.

The advantages of delegated budgets and semi-autonomous cost centres have to be balanced against the need to top-slice and cross-subsidize in order to implement the college mission. For example, to finance the estates strategy or for the provision of support services such as a nursery

Figure 3:   Estates strategy

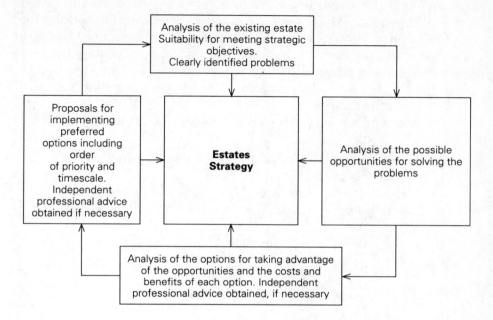

to improve access for particular groups in the community, or perhaps to protect and maintain high cost curriculum areas.

1.6   Estates Strategy

A fully integrated estates strategy includes:

- a condition survey report and accommodation strategy;
- a maintenance investment plan;
- a planned maintenance programme;
- suitable investment appraisal planning as well as the strategic issues illustrated in figure 3 above.

1.6.1   Accommodation Strategy

An accommodation strategy is a plan for the management and development of the estates which enables the college to deliver in a cost effective way, its academic objectives as specified in the strategic and operational plans.

The strategy should assess existing land and buildings against the strategic goals of the college, evaluate opportunities and options for rationalization and development, and set out a framework of priorities and timescales. In view of the value and costs of land and buildings and the lead times usually required to bring about developments of them, an accommodation strategy is a priority essential to the sound management of the college. It should be derived from the strategic objectives of the college.

In summary the accommodation strategy should identify:

- the existing estate, its suitability for meeting the strategic goals of the college, and its problems;
- the possible opportunities for solving the problems;
- the options for realizing opportunities, and their costs and benefits;
- the proposal for implementations, timing and order of priority.

1.6.2 Maintenance Investment Plan

The maintenance investment plan follows from the accommodation strategy and determines the type and level of maintenance appropriate for the college to invest in each part of its estate in the light of its strategic plan and accommodation strategy.

The maintenance investment plan determines the type and extent of maintenance which is justified for each building within the overall allocation of resources and the accommodation strategy in order to manage the estate most effectively.

The preparation of the accommodation strategy and its inter-relationship with a maintenance investment plan involves making choices which depend upon a number of variable factors. The information required to enable judgments to be made includes:

(i) the cost of putting the building into a serviceable condition. The conditions survey provides the basis of this information;

(ii) the cost of replacing the buildings with a new one. 'Architects' and 'quantity surveyors' services are needed;

(iii) the cost of replacing the building with another existing building. This involves exploring the locality for suitable premises to buy or rent and may require the retention of an agent to act for the college in the search;

(iv)   the value of the building or site in the market if it were sold for its most valuable use. The services of valuers experienced in the type of property and the market are needed here;

(v)   the costs of removal to alternative premises and the effect of disruption to activities;

(vi)   the disruptive effect on the use of the building of carrying out repair works.

1.6.3 Planned Maintenance Programme

The planned maintenance programme is a detailed, costed schedule preferably covering a ten-year period. It itemizes the maintenance and repair work that will be necessary or likely to be necessary to preserve the different parts of the estate in the condition identified by the maintenance investment plan as being consistent with the accommodation strategy and strategic plan of the college. It allows repairs and maintenance to be implemented according to agreed priorities so as to maximise the life and effectiveness of assets and to ensure that the works themselves are carried out efficiently.

Cost and quality of maintenance must be in balance with the financial and qualitative benefits maintenance brings to the college. The aims of a planned maintenance programme should be to:

(i)   provide a tool for budgeting and financial management;

(ii)   provide a means of relating programmed repair and maintenance works to other priorities such as refurbishment or redevelopment proposals and leasing policy;

(iii)   rectify major defects and restore fabric and services to an acceptable and safe condition;

(iv)   prevent major deterioration or failure in the fabric and services of the college and keep the assets in an acceptable condition;

(v)   preserve utility and, where appropriate, the value of the premises;

(vi)   maintain optimum performance of engineering services to ensure the internal environments and operational characteristics of the building are perceived at the correct levels;

(vii)   conduct repairs and maintenance over a period of years in a sensible sequence to reflect urgency of repair and permit efficiency of working and value for money;

(viii)   spread expenditure on maintenance evenly over a period of years where this is desirable.

1.6.4   Investment Appraisal

All proposals for significant capital expenditure need to be carefully appraised to determine which option offers the institution the best value for money when assessed against the strategic plan, accommodation strategy and maintenance investment plan. Detailed guidance is provided on the investment appraisal techniques approved by the Treasury for publicly-funded projects and on the factors which the Funding Council would expect to be taken into account in any such appraisal (see section 3.6).

1.7   Estates Management

The Estates Manager is responsible for managing the work necessary to ensure that the value of the college's estate is maintained, that sufficient suitable accommodation is provided for planned student numbers and that this accommodation is used effectively and efficiently for the maximum benefit of the college. These responsibilities are illustrated in figure 4.

Figure 4:   Estates management

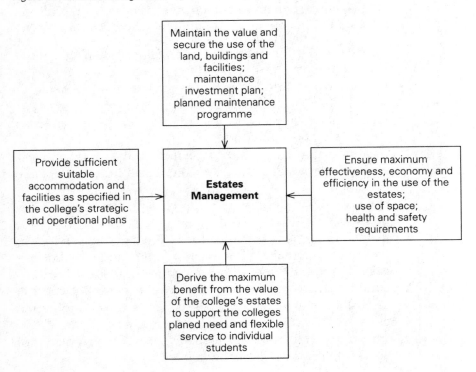

EXERCISE 1: Strategic and Operational Planning

Complete the following sections of this exercise, which will help you understand important facts, figures, strategies and objectives relating to your college.

1   Facts and figures
    (i)   Name of college ....
    (ii)   College mission statement ....
         ....
         ....
         ....
         ....

    (iii) Size of college
         (a)   Number of FEFC students ....
             Total number of students F/T .... P/T.................
             Distribution by age
             16–19 percentage.....................................%
             19–25 percentage.....................................%
             over 25 percentage ....%
             Total FTE students ....
             Total number of funding units ....
             Funding per unit 1993/94 ....
             Funding per unit 1994/95 ....
             Funding per unit 1995/96 ....
          (b)   Total budget...
             Percentage from FEFC ....
          (c)   Number of staff FTEs
             Teaching ....
             Support ....
          (d)   Number of sites ....
    (iv) Curriculum offer — Range of programmes
         for example, business studies

2   List the five main factors relating to your College which give rise to 'financial risk'
    (i)   ....
    (ii)   ....
    (iii)   ....
    (iv)   ....
    (v)   ....

3   Produce a summary Strengths Weaknesses Opportunities and Threats
    analysis for your college in the space below

Strengths	**Opportunities**
(i)	(i) ....
(ii)	(ii) ....
(iii)	(iii) ....
(iv)	(iv) ....

Weaknesses	**Threats**
(i)	(i) ....
(ii)	(ii) ....
(iii)	(iii) ....
(iv)	(iv) ....

4   On separate sheets of paper (using no more than one side of A4 for
    each) note what actions are being taken by your college to:
    (i)   maximize/increase the strengths
    (ii)   take advantage of the opportunities
    (iii)   deal with the weaknesses
    (iv)   manage and reduce the threats

5   List in order of priority and briefly describe your College's strategic
    objectives for the next three years
    (i)   ....
            ....
    (ii)   ....
            ....
    (iii)   ....
            ....
    (iv)   ....
            ....
    (v)   ....
            ....
    (vi)   ....
            ....
    (vii)   ....
            ....

(viii) ....
....

(ix) ....
....

(x) ....
....

6 Using the list that you have produced in 5 above, together with a copy of your college's strategic and operational plan, take each strategic objective in turn and check the extent to which it has been translated into concrete goals, expressed in terms which are measurable and can be checked as effective or otherwise and that they are costed and the timescale specified.

7 List the major strategic objectives of your college in respect of its estates/use of accommodation. Indicate timescale and estimates of total cost

(i) ....
....

(ii) ....
....

(iii) ....
....

(iv) ....
....

(v) ....
....

8 For each of the items listed in 7 above determine performance indicators that will show when the objective has been achieved.

(i) ....
....

(ii) ....
....

(iii) ....
....

(iv) ....
....

(v) ....
....

NOTES:

Financial Planning, Management and Control

2.1 Financial Planning

Financial planning plays a crucial role both in the process of strategic planning and in the process of monitoring and control. It involves quantifying the financial implications of plans, identifying and assessing possible financial strategies and monitoring expenditure against implementation budgets. Figure 5 illustrates the scope of financial planning.

2.2 The Financial Forecast

Financial forecasts are prepared on forms provided by the Further Education Funding Council and together with a commentary highlight the financial, ie revenue and capital, implications of changes in the strategic and operational plans.

The information contained in section 2.2 of this guide is adapted from FEFC Circular 94/15 *Financial Forecasts*. The forms used to complete the financial forecasts can also be found in this FEFC Circular.

2.2.1 Purpose of the Forecast

The financial forecast is intended to be a financial representation of the college's strategic plan. It allows each college to:

(i)   present to its management, board of governors and to the Funding Council a consolidated statement showing the cost and financial implications of fulfilling its plan;

(ii)   plan for its continued financial viability throughout the period of the plan;

(iii)   identify any pressure points which may impact significantly on the college's financial performance.

Figure 5: Financial planning

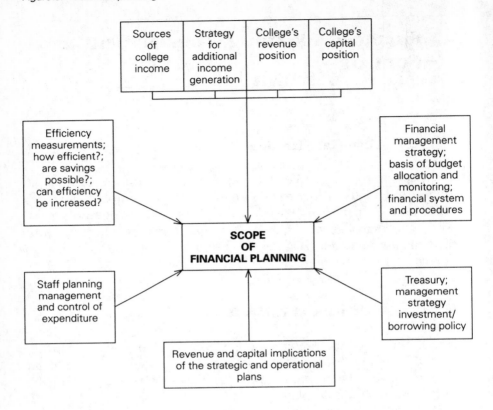

Sources of college income	Strategy for additional income generation	College's revenue position	College's capital position

Efficiency measurements; how efficient?; are savings possible?; can efficiency be increased?

Financial management strategy; basis of budget allocation and monitoring; financial system and procedures

SCOPE OF FINANCIAL PLANNING

Staff planning management and control of expenditure

Treasury; management strategy investment/ borrowing policy

Revenue and capital implications of the strategic and operational plans

2.2.2   The Scope of the Forecast

The forecast covers four accounting periods: the estimated out-turn for the present year, and the forecast for the next three years, and thus matches the period of the college's strategic plan. The forecast includes the following sections:

Form 1   —   Income
Form 2A   —   Non-pay expenditure
Form 2B   —   Pay expenditure
Form 3   —   Balance sheet
Form 4   —   Cashflow statement
Form 5   —   Sensitivity analysis
Form 6   —   Reconciliation of movements between years
Form 7   —   Principal's certificate

and, in addition, a commentary.

The commentary to support the forecast should provide a clear link between the strategic plan and the major assumptions or interpretations used. In particular, the commentary should explain significant changes in the figures from one year to the next.

2.2.3 Planning Assumptions

The reliability of the forecast clearly depends on the soundness of the underlying assumptions. The majority of the assumptions will flow from the college's strategic analysis and plan and the college is responsible for identifying and clearly communicating its own planning assumptions.

2.2.4 Completing the Forecast

When completing the forecast the following issues should be considered and included.

(i)   Statement of college's financial objectives:
  - the objectives should be consistent with those stated in the strategic plan;
  - the intended use of reserves should be indicated.

(ii) Statement of key assumptions:
  - include any information that aids understanding of the forecast financial statements;
  - indicate the general rate of inflation assumed in the forecast;
  - state any variation to the general inflation rate for any specific items of income or expenditure;
  - provide details of the college's approach to payroll costs;
  - indicate general trends in numbers employed and forecast future payment levels.

2.2.5 Supplementary Information Requested

Form 1 — Income

  - Provide a detailed explanation of all significant transfers to and from reserves.

- Include explanations of significant year-on-year movements.
- HE franchising — provide background information on the college links and basis of the contract.
- Identify the college's policy regarding subsidies for catering.
- Identify the colleges main income generating activities stating type of subsidy, if any.
- Identify any subsidiary companies listing name and the nature of business.

Form 2a and 2b — Non-pay and Pay Expenditure

- Provide details of any provisions included in the expenditure forecast.
- Give explanations of large year-on-year movements.
- Provide details of Hunter funds claimed analyzed into 'priority 1(a), 1(b), 2 and 3'.
- Provide details of any restructuring including listing the number of staff involved and reasons for the restructure.

Form 3 — Balance Sheet

- Provide a detailed explanation of provisions.
- Provide a detailed explanation of any restricted reserves.
- Identify significant asset purchases and disposals listing consents and purposes.
- Identify the depreciation policy for each category of assets.
- Provide a depreciation policy for each category of assets.
- Give an explanation of significant year-on-year movements in debtors and creditors.
- Give details of bad debts policy and provision.

Form 4 — Cashflow Statement

The cashflow statement will distinguish between the cash flows arising from the college's operating activities and the other inflows and outflows of cash resulting from investment and borrowing.

Form 5 — Sensitivity Analysis

The strategic analysis will identify possible future scenarios and critical factors that could cause the strategic and operational plans to vary. The plan and forecast therefore are based on a number of assumptions which may include the following.

- Inflation estimated.
- Estimates of national growth in further education.
- Estimates of expected funds from the Funding Council.
- Local authority policies and discretionary awards and transport.
- Competition from other providers of post-16 education.
- Terms and conditions of employment for college staff.
- Decline of major industries and employment prospects. An upturn in employment could have a significant effect on the achievement of growth targets.

In order to know how confident governors can be in relation to the planned position it will be necessary to subject the 'colleges' planned activities, income and expenditure to a 'what if' analysis. This involves considering the effect on outcomes and on the budget of various percentage changes to:

- income; (ie recurrent grant, educational contracts, tuition fees, etc)
- expenditure. (ie pay expenditure, non-pay expenditure, premises/estates expenditure, etc)

As much flexibility as possible should be built into the college's plans to increase the flexibility in the use of its resources to cope with changes in the profile of demand or of any of the other factors listed above. Contingency plans and portions of expenditure that could be shed in each forecast period, as necessary should be identified.

Form 6 — Reconciliation of Movements between Years

Since changes from one period to the next will be analyzed closely by people both inside and outside the college decisions made on the basis of the information and how it is presented will be crucial particularly in the early stages of incorporation.

Form 7 — Principal's Certificate

The forecasts are signed by the Principal to reinforce accountability.

2.3 Financial Management and Control

All colleges carry out a number of financial management activities that are necessary to maintain adequate control of financial affairs. All these activities are governed by the financial memorandum, financial regulations and financial procedures which provide clear and author-itative rules about who should do what in respect of the college's finances. In each of the financial areas the college's financial regula-tions and procedures establish controls and help protect the college from financial risk. These controls and procedures must be in place to ensure that:

- all financial regulations and procedures are complied with;
- any deviation from financial regulations and procedures is high-lighted promptly and effective corrective action is taken;
- there is adequate segregation of duties to prevent collusion and misappropriation;
- all financial transactions are recorded accurately and promptly;
- financial transactions are recorded in a way which allows use-ful analyses and reports to be produced;
- there is adequate budgetary control to ensure that expenditure is controlled within actual income levels;
- only authorized expenditure is incurred;
- all amounts owing to the institution are recorded accurately and collected promptly and the college is protected from the risk of bad debts;
- there is adequate physical control over the college's assets in-cluding cash, equipment, stock and buildings;
- loss from treasury mismanagement is prevented;
- investment decisions are fully informed and adequately appraised;
- the college is adequately protected and/or insured against all significant potential losses and risks;
- the legal and tax implications of all financial activities are con-sidered at the appropriate time;
- all financial transactions which occur are recorded in the accounts, and no transactions are recorded unless they have actually occurred;
- all transactions can, if necessary, be traced back, through an audit trail, to the original documents they reflect.

2.4 Budgeting and Management Accounts

Colleges need to establish budgets and produce management accounts and monitoring statements which help to ensure that progress towards the achievement of targets is satisfactory, that expenditure is controlled within actual income levels and that only authorized expenditure is incurred. All financial transactions must be recorded accurately and promptly (see Section Five).

2.5   Accounting Records

2.5.1   Within each college's financial services section proper books of accounts are kept with respect to:

- all money received and paid and the purpose to which it is applied;
- all sales and purchases;
- all assets and liabilities.

2.5.2   The financial memorandum between the Funding Council and the college states that the college shall provide the Council with audited accounts for the financial year (see specimen financial accounts, annex B).

2.6   Cashflow Management

Cash management is the process of determining and maintaining the proper level of cash within the college. The objective is to reduce to a minimum the cash balances in excess of the college's operating needs. The cash manager's activities include:

- cash collection — speeding up the collection and conversion of income into usable bank deposits;
- cash disbursement — controlling the outflow of payments;
- reducing or eliminating cash balances in excess of target balances and putting surplus cash to work by investing (for example, in the overnight money market);
- reducing or eliminating cash borrowing and keeping the amount of interest paid as low as possible.

The benefits of good cash management to a college include:

- better control of financial risk;
- opportunity for surplus income to be generated;
- increased confidence of FEFC, governors, staff, banks, etc.

The following systems and procedures should be in place to ensure that effective cashflow management is possible.

- All amounts owing to the college are recorded accurately and collected promptly and the risk of bad debts minimized.
- Colleges must know that cash resources will be available to meet obligations when they fall due.
- Payments to suppliers should be on the due date (not before) and any cash surpluses should be invested to earn the maximum amount of interest subject to the avoidance of undue risk.
- Any borrowing required should be obtained at competitive rates.
- Essential cash controls must be in place to ensure cash transactions are promptly and correctly recorded, cash is banked promptly and therefore, loss or theft avoided.

2.7 Treasury Management

Treasury management is the practice of cash investment and borrowing, the management and control of associated risks, and the achievement of the maximum return consistent with these risks. The aim when investing is to achieve the maximum return with the minimum risk and when borrowing the aim is to finance the project at minimum cost with the minimum (re)financing risk (see section 3.4).

2.8 Raising Capital/Capital Investment Proposal

Funding issues can be complex and it is important for the College to clearly understand what it is trying to achieve within the framework of the strategic and accommodation plans. The College should examine the risk factors and its cash flow situation when considering raising capital. Colleges need to prepare a capital investment proposal in order to demonstrate that the project for which capital is required is really necessary (see section 3.6 for what to include in a capital investment proposal).

2.9 Purchasing

Central control over purchasing and payments makes effective financial control possible (see section 3.2). This will ensure that:

- goods and services are ordered at competitive prices;
- the purchase is correctly documented, authorized, included in the budget and appropriate;
- there are adequate funds to meet the commitment;
- the impact upon the college's profit and loss account and cash flow can be recorded immediately;
- payments are made on the due date for goods and services actually received.

2.10 Payroll

Proper management of the payroll is critical to the effective financial management and control of the college (see section 3.3). However this is done all deductions in respect of tax, national insurance, pensions and any other obligations must be correctly accounted for and payments made on the due date to the appropriate authorities. Valid employees of the college must be paid the correct amounts on the right day and the college must know in advance that the expectation of what should be paid in total to all employees in any given month tallies with the total of actual payments to be made before the payroll is run.

2.11 Fixed Assets

2.11.1 Fixed Asset Register

The College will have in place a Fixed Asset Register with effective financial controls and procedures to ensure that:

- the assets included in the college's balance sheet are physically there and are secure against damage and theft;
- the college's profit and loss account is charged the correct amount of depreciation to reflect the reduction in value of the college's equipment and other assets;
- all the college's fixed assets, above an agreed value, are included in the college's balance sheet at the correct value.

2.11.2 Equipment Replacement Programmes

In its Circular 93/10 the FEFC advises colleges which have not already done so to establish equipment replacement policies and a rolling equipment replacement programme. These enable a college to increase its purchasing power and coordinate its equipment replacement programme with its building refurbishment programme. Colleges are free to vire money from revenue to capital if they wish to assist the funding of such programmes.

2.11.3   Depreciation Policy

Depreciation should conform to the best accounting practice as set out in the Companies Act, statements of standard accounting practice (SSAPs) — accounting for depreciation.

The treatment as a revenue expense of capital expenditure items using the concept of materiality and a cut-off value for capitalization at £500 per item or at any other level acceptable to the college's auditors. The cut-off value should be set only after discussion with the college auditor.

Items of capital expenditure should be depreciated in line with generally accepted accounting practice and depreciation rates may in practice vary between colleges. The depreciation policy should be disclosed by way of a note to the accounts.

2.12   Insurance

The governing body is responsible for securing adequate insurance cover for all risks associated with the running of the College. The main risk is for loss of buildings and equipment through fire and theft but cover is necessary for employers liability, governors liability, third party and vehicles. To arrange insurance there are three stages: first to assess the risk, secondly to design a strategy to cover those risks and thirdly to obtain cover at the best price to respond to those risks. The adequacy of cover should be reviewed on a regular basis and comparative quotations obtained.

2.13   Taxation

As charities, colleges do not have to pay tax on many of their activities but will be registered and have controls to ensure that:

- proper records are maintained to ensure that the right amount of tax (PAYE, VAT, Corporation Tax or local taxes) is paid at the right time;

- returns and payments are made as required by the fiscal authorities;
- the college does not incur unnecessary tax liabilities, for example on income from the provision of commercial services.

2.14 The Audit

The role of internal audit is to provide the college management with an objective assessment of whether systems and controls are working properly and, as such, is a key part of the college's internal control systems. The main objective of external audit is to report on the truth and fairness of the financial situation of the college and assure that the required statistical data has been accurately compiled (see Section 3.7).

2.15 Planning of Staffing

2.15.1 Staff Planning

Staff planning should enable the college to make the best use of its existing staff and meet the existing needs for staffing identified in the strategic and operational plans. Staffing accounts for between 70 and 80 per cent of the college's revenue budget and is, therefore, one of the most important elements of financial planning. Future staffing needs must also be predicted and provided for within the financial plan. Managers will need to consider the factors illustrated in figure 6, if staff planing is to be effective.

2.15.2 Recruitment and Selection Procedures

The personnel policy should set out clearly the College's arrangements for recruitment and selection. An example of a college recruitment process is shown in figure 7, and an example of an appointment procedure or selection process is shown in figure 8a and 8b.

Figure 6: Planning of staffing

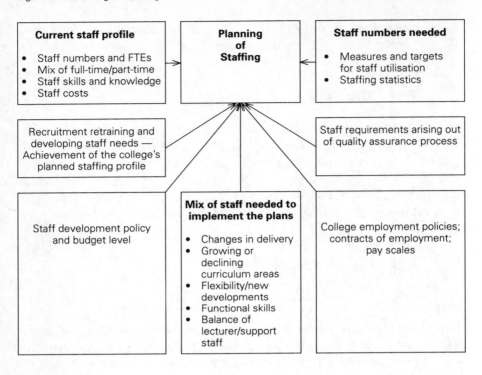

Figure 7:   The recruitment process

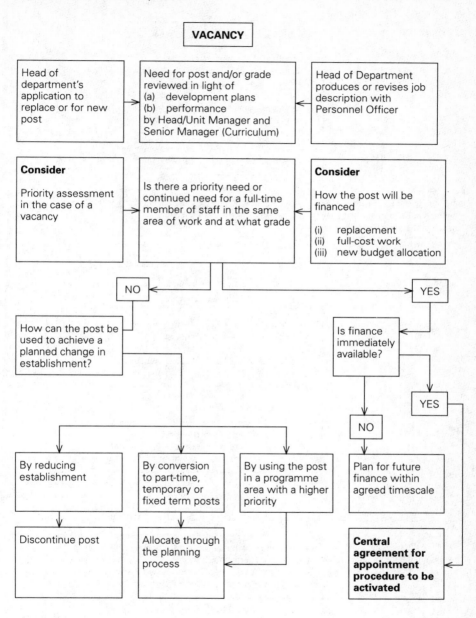

Figure 8a: *Appointment procedure*

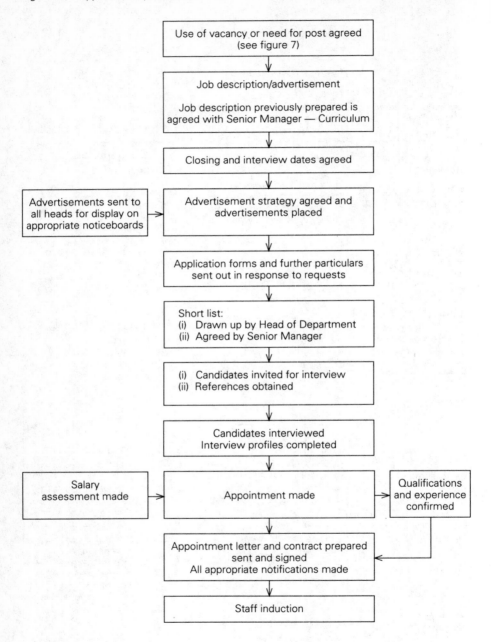

Figure 8b: Part-time staff contracts: control spreadsheets produced monthly

Each academic department will have established its total programme hour requirement for the period and determined the total workload in hours for which academic staff will be needed. Academic planning will have identified the level of work to be undertaken by part-time staff and authorization given for the issue of part-time staff contracts. The following spreadsheets provide examples of part-time staff monitoring statements.

1 Summary cumulative grand totals by month (hours/grade/cost)
   This spreadsheet shows the month-by-month commitment to part-time staff contracts on a whole college basis.

Month/ hour	Grade 5 Hours	Grade 4 Hours		Grade 1 Hours	Total Hours	Total Cost
Aug.						
Sept.						
Oct.						
July						
Total hours						
Total cost						

2 Summary cumulative totals by department (hours/grade/cost)
   This spreadsheet shows similar information but is ordered by department.

Dept/hour	Grade 5 Hours	Grade 4 Hours		Grade 1 Hours	Total Hours	Total Cost
Business studies						
Construction						
Creative studies						
Science						
Total hours						
Total cost						

   Note: Many colleges pay one grade, some two only etc, to part-time staff and do not use the five grades indicated in the example above.

3 Analysis by department/staff name/hours/cost
   This spreadsheet provides much more detailed information at the level of the individual member of staff.

Department	Staff type	Pay ref	Surname	Initials	Hours	Rate grade	Total cost	Month
Business	FT	014/ 9871	Brown	RI	214	4		Oct.
Business	FT	014/ 3214	West	GH	108	5		Oct.
Business	PT	101/ 849	White	NB	304	1		Oct.
Science	PT	010/ 674	Green	BJ	189	4		June
Totals								

2.16 Information Requirements for Financial Planning

The college will have considered its management information needs at all levels so that it could define its management information requirements. The definition of requirements is not easy because colleges are having to make assumptions about their information needs at a time of rapid change and against the background of external requirements. The college's management information systems strategy must be built upon the information needs of the college and the use of an interrelational database, not built around hardware or software restrictions or a system that relates to one information requirement only. It is essential that when colleges are developing management information systems sufficient investment is made in both staffing and equipment and the speed of development controlled at a level at which that college can manage to maintain the accuracy and credibility of outputs. The information requirements for financial planning are illustrated in figure 9 below.

Figure 9: Financial planning information

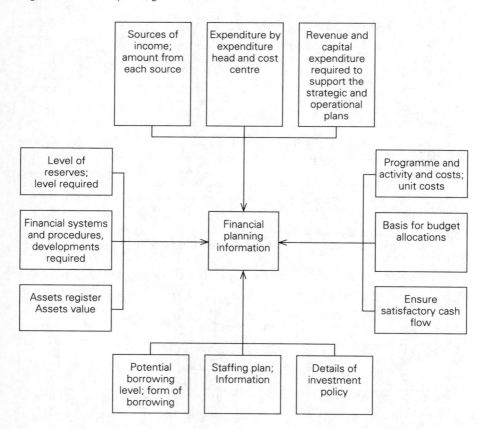

EXERCISE 2: Financial Planning Management and Control

Complete this exercise to improve your understanding of your college's financial planning management and control systems.

1   Preparation:
    (i)   Obtain and read a copy of your college's Financial Regulations and Financial Procedures.
    (ii)   Obtain and read copies of all the audit reports produced during the past eighteen months. Note any weaknesses identified and the management responses and actions taken.
    (iii)   Obtain or draw up an organization chart of your college's Financial Services section indicating the main duties of each post.

2   List the five most significant assumptions made in preparing your college's Financial Forecasts and briefly describe the action the College would take in the case of a worst scenario situation occurring.
    (i)   ....
            ....
            ....
            ....
    (ii)   ....
            ....
            ....
            ....
    (iii)   ....
            ....
            ....
            ....
    (iv)   ....
            ....
            ....
            ....
    (v)   ....
            ....
            ....
            ....

3   Using section 2.2.4 as a checklist consider the extent to which your college has covered the issues shown in preparing its Financial Forecasts.

4 Using headings only list in priority order the information requirements of your college for financial planning at both college and
departmental level.

College level	**Departmental level**
(i)	(i) ....
(ii)	(ii) ....
(iii)	(iii) ....
(iv)	(iv) ....
(v)	(v) ....

5 Briefly describe your college's system for staff planning monitoring
and control in respect of both full-time and part-time staff.

6 Obtain and read your college's equipment replacement policy. List
its main features.

(i)   ....
       ....
(ii)   ....
       ....
(iii) ....
       ....
(iv)   ....
       ....
(v)   ....
       ....

7 Obtain a copy of your college's 'Depreciation Policy' consider the
treatment of depreciation in your year-end accounts. Prepare a short
paper of no more than one side of A4 explaining the concept of
depreciation in a way that would easily be understood by any
member of staff in the college.

8 Consider how your college manages its cash flow, using section
2.6.3 and past audit reports relating to cash flow check the systems
and procedures are in place in your college and obtain copies of
monitoring reports produced.

9 Obtain a copy of your college's year-end report and accounts. List
ten factors which you consider are the most important and significant based on the financial and other information included.

NOTES:

Business Functions and Services

3.1 Introduction

This section of the guide covers major business functions and services essential for sound financial management and the business operation in the college. It is divided into the following sections:

- Obtaining value for money through the college purchasing function;
- Managing a payroll service and putting in place a college payroll disaster recovery plan;
- Treasury management;
- Considering capital investment and preparing a capital investment proposal;
- Managing the audit and preparing an audit plan.

3.2 College Purchasing Function — Obtaining Value for Money

3.2.1 Objectives

The objectives of a college purchasing function are as follows.

(i) Ensuring that all goods and services are purchased at the most economical prices available while ensuring that the quality and standard of goods and services meets college specifications.

(ii) Establishing a database containing information on purchasing patterns at college and departmental level which will act as an aid to purchasing policy/strategy.

(iii) Providing on-line purchasing information to cost centre managers.

(iv) Monitoring purchasing both at a college and departmental level to ensure that purchasing conforms to college Financial Regulations and purchasing procedures.

(v) Increasing awareness throughout the college of the need to plan purchasing in order to produce further cost savings. The co-ordination of purchasing requirements which leads to a bulk order being placed for supplies should result in bulk purchase discounts.

The maintenance of a central database containing information on college and departmental purchasing patterns will indicate the overall cost savings by departments and provide essential information on cost monitoring etc. The coordinated planning of purchasing will also enable the college to exercise complete control over the incidence of expenditure and in turn will aid cash flow monitoring and management.

3.2.2 Obtaining Value for Money

(i) Purchasing policy
  • A college needs a corporate purchasing policy and purchasing and supply procedures. Amongst other things the policy should ensure that no invoices are paid sooner than is necessary to meet credit terms or secure discounts.
  • The purchasing policy should require the use of competitive quotations. There should also be a requirement to seek tenders when minimum value limits are exceeded. Those procedures relating to European law should be particularly well defined.
  • For most colleges the services of a Consortium for Purchasing and Distribution is necessary because its own purchasing capacity will be insufficient to obtain the best prices. The college should also have a computer facility which permits both on-line ordering and access to a purchasing catalogue. This will also assist in the achievement of the objectives listed at 3.2.1.

(ii) The purchasing process
  The ordering, commitment and purchasing process should be computerized and fully integrated with the College's management and financial reporting systems. A decentralized process with centralized monitoring and control procedures can provide the most effective style of procurement management.

(iii) Purchasing practice
Significant savings can be made if someone with training and experience of purchasing within the college acts as a Purchasing Officer. It is desirable that the college should use standard terms and conditions for all purchases and ensure that all orders are raised on a printed order form.

Savings are possible if the college operates a minimum order value policy and the management information system enables expenditure to be categorized by:

- product or service group (for example, stationery or engineering materials);
- supplier;
- purchaser.

Consideration of the most appropriate stores procedure and knowledge of the value of stock held and issued during each financial period are necessary.

(iv) Accountability within the purchasing system
Careful consideration is necessary of the number of individuals in the college authorized to select suppliers and sign purchase orders. The smaller the number the easier it is to arrange appropriate training in required skills (for example, negotiation skills).

3.3 Managing a Payroll Service and Putting in Place a College Payroll Disaster Recovery Plan

3.3.1 Payroll Management

Proper management of the payroll is critical to the effective financial management and control of the college. Figure 10 below illustrates the scope of payroll management.

3.3.2 Disaster Recovery

Deductions in respect of tax, national insurance, pensions and any other obligations must be correctly accounted for and payments made on the due date to the appropriate authorities. Valid employees of the

Figure 10:   *Payroll in education*

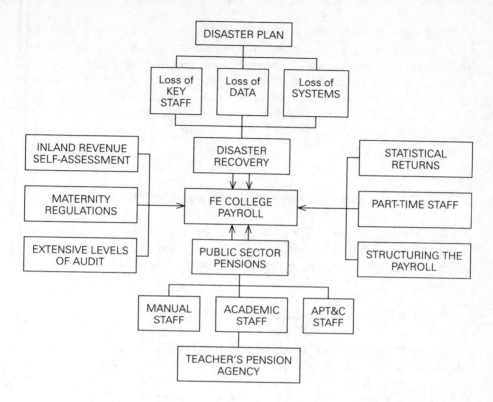

Figure 11:   *Payroll disaster recovery diagram*

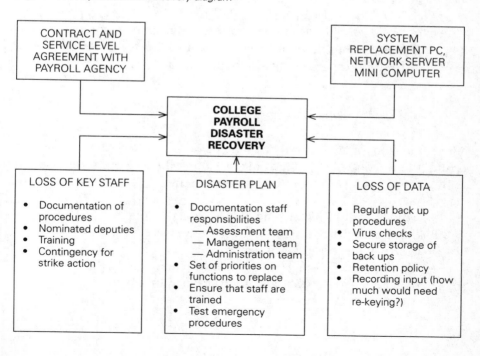

college must be paid the correct amounts on the right day and the college must know in advance that the expectation of what should be paid in total to all employees in any given month tallies with the total of actual payments to be made before the payroll is run, ie gross to gross reconciliations should be carried out each month. It is important that the College has a payroll disaster recovery plan in place which will cope in the event of a system failure. Figure 11 below illustrates the extent of such a plan.

3.4 Treasury Management in Further Education

Treasury management is the practice of cash investment and borrowing, the management and control of associated risks, and the achievement of the maximum return consistent with these risks.

3.4.1 Trustee Investment Act 1961

Under section 19(4)(d) of the Further and Higher Education Act 1992, further education corporations are given the power to invest any sums of money not immediately required for the purposes of carrying out their lawful activities. When exercising this power, all colleges are subject to the Trustee Investment Act 1961, section 2.

A copy of the Act can be obtained from Her Majesty's Stationery Office and colleges should ensure that their investments comply within its provisions. Further guidance relevant to the Trustee Investment Act 1961 can be found in Funding Council Circular 93/13.

3.4.2 Treasury Management Risks

While the aim of treasury management is to achieve the maximum return, the risks involved, which include the following, must be considered and every effort made to minimize them:

- risk of loss of all or part of the capital sum;
- not maximizing interest on investments;
- not paying too much interest on loans;
- liquidity-not having cash available when required;
- legality-ensuring that all the 'rules' are followed;
- fraud.

3.4.3   Coping with Treasury Risks

In order to minimize risk the Treasury Manager will consider a number of factors which include the following:

- diversification;
- interest exposure management;
- cashflow forecasting;
- maturity profile.

3.4.4   Investing

The aim when investing is to achieve the maximum return with the minimum risk. The key questions to ask when investing are:

- How much cash is available?
- When is it available?
- When will it be needed?
- What are the investment objectives?
- What legal/practical constraints are there?

There are three main approaches which can be used by a college to manage investments;

- entirely in-house;
- in-house using brokers/advisers;
- external cash managers.

3.4.5   Interest Rate Risk Management

Interest rates change from time to time and the Treasury Manager will wish to ensure a portfolio of investments in order that the maximum rate of interest and therefore return on the investment is achieved. This will include consideration of the following:

- clear policies;
- reliable cashflow forecasting;
- dependable external advice;
- sound exposure measurement system;

- familiarity with hedging techniques;
- interest rate variables.

3.4.6   Controlling the Risk to the Capital Sum

It is essential that any capital sum being invested is not at risk and the Treasury Manager will exercise control through the following:

- approved list of borrowers/limits;
- approved investment instruments;
- understanding credit assessment;
- use of credit ratings;
- knowledge of 'unrated' borrowers.

3.4.7   What You Need to Know about a Company before Investing (Credit Consideration)

The college needs to be sure that any money it invests is safe. One way to minimize risk is to know certain key information about the company through which the investments will be made. The information required include:

- balance sheet strength;
- liquidity;
- financial history;
- borrowing ability;
- size/period.

3.4.8   Review Your Banking Relationship

Each college should ensure that their partnership with their bank is cost effective and forms a part of an integrated money transmission and treasury management process. It is important to keep the partnership under review so that value for money is obtained from the bank related costs. The bank will be able to work with the college to borrow money to finance a project when necessary. The aim when borrowing is to finance the project at minimum cost with the minimum (re)financing risk.

3.4.9 *Preparing a Treasury Policy Statement*

Every college should give careful consideration to treasury management and the communication of policy to all staff who are involved.
The preparation of a Treasury Policy Statement including the following
is necessary:

- approved investments/limits;
- approved brokers/advisors;
- approved forms of borrowing;
- approved lenders;
- policy on investment rate exposure;
- delegation to committees/officers;
- reporting arrangements;
- clearing banking arrangements.

3.4.10 *Preparing a Treasury Systems and Procedures Document*

Arising from the policy statement the necessary systems and associated
procedures should be documented. Matters to be included should
include:

- delegation of treasury functions;
- procedures for preparing and monitoring cash flow projections;
- dealing procedures;
- the use of brokers;
- the evidencing of deals;
- money transmission procedures;
- limits to decision-making;
- reporting arrangements and frequency.

3.5 Investing in the Estate — Land and Buildings

Many colleges of further education will be considering a substantial
investment to upgrade their buildings. The buildings on the site of
some colleges are in a poor state of repair and sometimes spread over
a number of sites, whereas for other colleges their problem is to accom-
modate planned increases in student numbers.

It is likely that these colleges will have considered four main options:

- to remodel existing buildings;
- to demolish one or more existing buildings and rebuild;
- to dispose of one or more existing sites and either move to a new site(s);
- or build on existing sites.

Whatever options are considered, funding will be sought increasingly from the capital markets on a pre-planned basis rather than, as in the past by reliance on 'one-off funding' from traditional sources. Not all colleges will qualify for such funding nor will all wish to seek it but, clearly, there is a need for a balanced approach to capital funding which has the ability to offer flexible funding schemes and which properly weighs the wishes of the college against its financial abilities.

3.5.1 Further Education Funding Council (FEFC)

The Funding Council operates a very strict vetting procedure over colleges in the funding of property development. In terms of academic accommodation the council requires evidence that the purpose of the development is shown within the college's strategic plan and estates strategy, that the project is necessary, optimizes space utilization, is affordable and does represent value for money. In terms of residential accommodation the proposed development must also fall within the college's estates strategy, be self-financing, not impact adversely on education services, stand a 10 per cent sensitivity test, and not cause the college to pass the interest cost watershed (ie 7 per cent of gross income) and pass the current net present value (NPV) test requirement.

The Funding Council should receive any proposal from the college at as early a stage as possible. They examine the documentation very carefully and any possible inconsistencies which cannot be explained result in the proposal being returned.

3.5.2 Development Value

The college is likely, for accounting purposes, to have utilized a valuation method known as depreciated replacement cost. This is the current cost of replacing the asset depreciated over the remaining life of the building at the date of valuation. It has no regard to the true, open market, value of the development which, in any case, is almost certainly built under restricted planning permission allied to the provision of education. It is, therefore, extremely important to look at the true meaning of security value requirements when considering educational funding packages. Three examples of typical funding packages are considered below.

(i) Bank advances invariably come from a negotiated deal with the bank based on the covenant strength of the college and on the bank's ability to 'trawl' for additional security and/or to get the college to agree that it will maintain certain status, gearing or results. If the college does not maintain its pledge the loan can be immediately called. Critically, the pledge may tie the college to not negotiating other debts without the prior approval of the bank. Another possible clause could include the college not altering its constitution without first conferring with the bank. Clearly this could provide the college with an additional restraint during a time of change.

(ii) Finance lease transactions are less prone to security values except that leasing companies will often call for an open market value of at least as much as the advance. This could also bring into question additional security or possible negative pledges.

(iii) Capital market funding looks primarily at covenant strength and any shortfall in security values would be addressed by lease extensions and/or amortization of capital over the term of the issued lease.

3.5.3 *Covenant Value*

The covenant value of a college is in reality a subjective test of its ability to service a debt or lease. Accordingly, covenant value does not purely judge the underlying asset base of a college but also brings into the equation its operating results, its budgetary and financial management, its cash flow indicators and its general strategic position within its market.

Most funding or investing institutions have certain individual target values to initiate a covenant test. These may include limitations on advances as a percentage of net worth (often 25–33 per cent), the degree to which budgeted cashflow surpluses cover debt or lease servicing (often between 1.5 and 2.5 times cover) and the net liquidity or quick liquidity which is maintained by the college (the degree to which quickly available assets cover immediate debts).

3.5.4 Taxation Implications

Generally colleges are not liable to taxation and are exempt or partially exempt for VAT purposes. This gives rise to both advantages and disadvantages.

As a non-tax paying body certain allowances, inherent in property development, cannot be utilized by the college as they have no taxable profit against which to set them. The use of intermediary tax paying bodies to utilize allowances can effect a reduction in cost of debt servicing by reducing original cost by a percentage of the net present value of tax allowances claimable by the intermediary. Such allowances may include capital allowances on plant and fixtures, industrial buildings allowances and lease premium relief.

As an exempt, as opposed to zero rated, VAT body a college will be hit for VAT on development costs as an up front capital cost.

Proper planning of a development, prior to its commencement, is vital in these aspects and can have a marked effect on debt evaluation.

3.5.5 Conclusion

Funding issues are complex and it is important to understand clearly the college's objectives, not just in respect of the immediate project but within the framework of the strategic and accommodation (or estates) plans. Borrowing has an impact both on the college's own balance sheet and its available security to pledge against future borrowings. It is vital that the college does not enter into a transaction now which precludes future financing of projects which may have more long-term benefits to the college and its planned growth. It is important to consider if the project is really necessary and if the new building will generate savings. Possible difficulties in the event of changes in interest rates within the general context of the economic environment should be considered and the college should examine the risk factor involved and its cash flow situation.

3.6 What to Include in a Capital Investment Proposal

The Further Education Funding Council requires the following information to be included in any capital investment proposal sent to them. This section draws heavily from the FEFC support package supplied to colleges.

3.6.1 College Need

Additional accommodation is required to . . .
Summary of existing accommodation and its condition.

3.6.2 Options

The following options have been considered:

Option 1   Purchase
Option 2   Lease
Option 3   Purpose built
Option 4   No increase

3.6.3 Purchase of Property — Option 1

(i)   What, where, what it would be used for.
(ii)   Summary of costs:
   • capital, for example, purchase price, furniture cost;
   • revenue, for example, annual staff cost, annual running costs.
(iii)   Proposed finance package:
   • bank loan;
   • college reserves;
   • Hunter condition survey savings.
(iv)   Advantages and disadvantages of this option.

3.6.4 Lease of a Property — Option 2

(i)   What, where, what it would be used for.
(ii)   Summary of costs:

- capital (for example, furniture cost);
- revenue (for example, annual staff cost, annual running cost, annual rent)

(iii) Advantages and disadvantages of this option.

3.6.5 Purpose Built Development — Option 3

(i)   Where, size, what it would be used for.
(ii) Summary of costs.
(iii) Proposed finance package.
(iv) Advantages:
- Purpose-built property.
- New property hence lower maintenance cost.
- Is further development of the site possible?
- Ease of access.

(v)   Disadvantages.

3.6.6 No Increase in Buildings — Option 4

(i)   Advantages
(ii) Disadvantages

3.6.7 Project Evaluation

(i)   Net present value (NPV) and cash flows
      Include a net present value calculation (NPV) and cash flow projection for each option over a period of twenty-five years and indicate at what rate they have been discounted.

Summary of New Present Value

Options	NPV (£)
1 Purchase	
2 Lease	
3 Purpose-built	
4 No increase	

(ii) Preferred Option

State which option produces the highest NPV over the twenty-five year period at the discounted rate chosen. State again the purpose and reason for the proposal and why the particular option is preferred.

3.6.8   Sensitivity Analysis

Evaluation

Investment appraisal reports should be produced for each option and these should contain sensitivity analysis of changes in cost and income of 20 per cent. When the preferred option is established a more detailed sensitivity analysis should be carried out on this. To do this it is necessary to determine a number of critical cost/income areas, for example, capital costs, annual expenditure, income from students. The amount by which costs could increase or income decrease in respect of each critical area from the levels shown before the net present value becomes negative should be determined.

3.6.9   Summary

Colleges should aim to demonstrate that the net present value of the preferred option is robust and that substantial increases in costs or decreases in income would be required before the NPV becomes negative and that this is unlikely.

3.6.10   Market Research/Evidence of Need

Demonstrate that market research has been undertaken to ensure adequate demand and explain the implications of the status quo.

3.6.11   Dealing with the Work Scenario

Although the sensitivity analysis should show that the preferred option is reasonably robust to fluctuations in cost and income, the proposal should also indicate what actions you would take in the worst scenario situation.

3.6.12 Some of the Tasks to be Undertaken before Implementation

These include:

- governors' approval;
- detailed plans, cash flow projections, net present value calculations and proposed finance method for each option;
- confirmation in writing of bank loan or any grants required;
- planning permission, if required;
- Further Education Funding Council approval;
- tenders;
- legal aspects of the project.

3.7 The Audit Function

3.7.1 The Role and Objectives of Internal and External Audit

(i) Internal Audit
The role of internal audit is to provide the college management with an objective assessment of whether systems and controls are working properly and, as such, it is a key part of the college's internal control systems. Although directed towards the financial systems of the college, the internal control systems also embrace the notion of achieving value for money and internal audit will address those sorts of issues also. It is clear that the audit function is crucial to the effective management of the college but internal audit is not an extension or a substitute for the functions of the college management. It is one of the ways in which the college can ensure appropriate review and evaluation of its systems.

(ii) External Audit
The basic objective of external auditors is to report on the truth and fairness of the financial situation of the college and any subsidiary companies which are shown in the financial statements. In addition there are certain statistical returns which have a direct bearing on the college's funding and, therefore, have to be certified by external auditors to ensure that the Funding Council and the college can be assured that such statistical data have been accurately compiled.

From the above, it is obvious that a clear relationship exists between internal and external audit and the work of these two bodies is related, in part, to different aspects of the corporation's operation. In providing certification that the college's financial returns are both true and fair, the work of the external auditors will have a direct impact upon the Finance Committee since, although that body is responsible for recommending all aspects of major financial import to the corporation, those governors as a group need to be assured nonetheless that the statements of financial accounts brought before them have been prepared accurately. Internal audit is related much more closely to the Audit Committee since the role of internal audit is to provide advice on management controls of which the work of the Finance Committee is a part. The college also needs to take account of the role which the full corporation has to play in these matters. There are certain matters for which the corporation takes full responsibility and these include the approval of annual estimates of income and expenditure, the efficient and effective use of resources, the solvency of the college and the corporation and the safeguarding of assets.

3.7.2 How to Carry out an Audit Needs Assessment

The assessment should:

- identify all areas of work within the organization by examining systems and sub-systems and group them together for internal audit purposes;
- assess the risk and priority of each area of work;
- determine a two to five-year cycle over which all systems would be audited.

Identification of Areas of Work

Budgets can be used to identify which financial areas are most suitable to include in the audit plan. The budgets also identify college departments and the audit needs assessment will take account of the fact that some financial systems operate and are controlled at departmental level. The audit work will also cover processing systems namely general ledger, debtors and cash collection, creditor payments, fixed assets, petty cash and budgetary control.

Assessment of Risk

The parameters used to determine the risk factor, and so determine the number of allocated days necessary for the audit, are as follows:

When deciding how many audit days are required a risk assessment is necessary within clearly defined parameters. The different income streams and/or expenditure is given a 'materiality' factor and ranked using a scale of 0 to 10 ranging from low to high risk. This factor ranges from a low ranking for petty cash to a high ranking for payroll.

The 'quality' of the system parameter ranges from a low ranking for FEFC income and general ledger where fewer risks are perceived to a high ranking for departmental expenditure and non grant income where the greatest risks are perceived.

The 'concerns' parameter ranges from a low ranking for FEFC income, petty cash and general ledger to a high ranking for payroll, departmental expenditure, non-grant income and maintenance expenditure.

This is coupled with a knowledge and experience of the college and the sector.

The above factors need to be weighted in order to determine the overall risk factor. The weighting used can be for example:

- Materiality — 40%
- Quality of system — 25%
- Concerns — 35%

The risk factors are then applied using a computer model to determine the number of allocated audit days to each area. In terms of the audit cycle, it is proposed that all core systems are covered each year, with other systems and academic departments being covered in a one to four-year cycle depending on the nature of the item.

3.7.3 The Audit Plan

Components of the Audit Plan

The plan shows the total number of man days for each period and has a number of component parts:

(i) Core financial systems form the main part of the audit plan. It is vitally important that these key systems are working satisfactorily so sufficient days need to be allocated to provide comfort to management. The number of days reduces in subsequent years, reflecting the reduced risk associated with them.

(ii)   Other systems/academic services cover the main non-core activities and will be covered largely on a cyclical basis.
(iii) Departmental reviews test a variety of systems which operate at a departmental level, such as ordering controls, budgetary controls and inventory control. These will be covered over a three-year cycle.
(iv) For each year, man days can be included for system efficiency studies.
(v)   The administrative computer audit focuses on both the overall management information systems control such as computer security arrangements and the operational processing controls.
(vi) Contracts audits will be required particularly when major capital projects are proposed.

3.7.4   Audit Timetable

The audit timetable divides the internal audit plan into three main segments. The first segment can include interim testing on the core systems, the computer audit, the first departmental reviews and some work on other systems.

The second segment can include the testing of the tuition fees and enrolment and the start of efficiency audits.

The third segment follows up on the interim testing to ensure that the key systems continue to operate satisfactorily providing the necessary comfort to the external auditors. It can also include the other remaining systems and departmental reviews.

EXERCISE 3: Business Functions and Services

Explore your college's business functions and services by completing this exercise.

1 Contracted-in Business Services — At What Cost?
  (i) Complete the table below for your college inserting against each service expected and actual costs.
  (ii) Provide details and comment on the variances in each case.

Name of service	Tender price quotation	Annual budget established	Actual annual expenditure	Variance
Insurance				
Treasury-1-Banking				
-2-Other				
Audit -1-Internal				
-2-External				
-3-Other				
Payroll				
Legal				
Purchasing				
Executive leasing — Refectory				
Other consultancy				
Other business services				
TOTALS				

2 Investigate the effectiveness of your college's purchasing regulations and procedures and the extent to which purchasing is planned in order to obtain value for money.

3 (i) Consider how your college manages its payroll service under the headings shown in this guide (figure 10). Check that your

college has control mechanisms and information flow checks in place relating to the division of responsibility between the payroll service, the Personnel Service and the Financial Services sections.

(ii) Check the extent to which a disaster recovery plan is in place.

4 Obtain a copy of your college's 'Treasury Policy' and consider the extent to which in respect of both cash investment and borrowing it manages and controls risk and the achievement of the maximum return consistent with risk.

5 Obtain, read and understand your college's estates strategy and consider the extent to which it:
   (i) supports the achievement of the objectives in the college's strategic and operational plans;
   (ii) covers the scope of the strategy illustrated in figure 3 of this guide.

6 With reference to section 3.7 — The Audit Function — carry out your own audit needs assessment for your college and produce an appropriate audit plan.

NOTES:

Income and Expenditure

4.1 Introduction — Sources and Uses of Funds

The financial memorandum produced by the Further Education Funding Council states that a college's total income must be sufficient, taking one year with another, to meet its total expenditure. This section of the guide covers the main sources of income and items of expenditure of a college and the factors that influenced this.

Colleges will be working to obtain the maximum value for the income they earn from whatever source in order that they can carry out as many as possible of their planned activities necessary for the achievement of their objectives. To do this the college will want to know at as detailed a level as possible their income streams and will have established the revenue and capital expenditure implications of their strategic and operational plans.

Figure 12 illustrates the main items of income and expenditure. These items will provide the basis for the income and expenditure account of the college which will also deal with and relate to all the activities of the college under the accruals concept of accounting.

4.2 Income from the Further Education Funding Council

4.2.1 *The Further Education Funding Council Provides Four Different Types of Funding for Colleges:*

(i)   the main recurrent funding allocations for college running costs which includes the demand-led element relating to enrolments and retention of students;

(ii) capital allocations which it allocates to colleges for expenditure under three categories:
   • equipment;
   • minor works;
   • major projects;

Figure 12: Income & expenditure

INCOME

- revenue grants from the FEFC;
- capital grants from the FEFC;
- tuition fees for further education courses;
- funding by TECs;
- contract income and tuition fees for short courses, higher education, schools and other directly funded provision;
- recurrent funding by the HEFCE/HEFCW/SHEFC/DENI;
- consultancy and other income from the sale of expertise and services;
- income generated by residential accommodation, catering and conferences;
- grants from the European Union and government departments;
- gifts and donations;
- farm income in agricultural colleges.

EXPENDITURE

- staffing;
- materials and equipment (books and other teaching materials, consumables, equipment and reprographics);
- premises running costs (repairs and maintenance, energy, a proportion of non-domestic rates, rents, cleaning, grounds and estates, security, laundry, linen and other domestic services);
- travel, subsistence and other expenses;
- establishment expenses (office furniture and equipment, telephones, printing, postage, insurance);
- professional and agency fees (audit fee, bank charges, legal fees, payroll costs);
- advertising, publicity and marketing;
- curriculum expenses (examination fees, external examiners' fees);
- student union association grant;
- insurance;
- interest payable;
- charges stemming from operating leases;
- irrecoverable value added tax.

(iii) funds paid to compensate colleges for specific types of expenditure, for example, restructuring;

(iv) funds which may only be applied to certain objectives, for example, access funds, funds for external institutions.

4.2.2 Recurrent Funding Method of Allocation

One of the main aims of the FEFC process for funding colleges is to fund the process of learning or units of activity supporting learning, rather than following the previous practice of the funding of teaching which depended on counts of full-time equivalent (FTE) student numbers. Key features of the new approach are as follows:

(i)   a block allocation to each college to be used as the college wishes within the framework of a financial memorandum from the Council;

(ii) a funding agreement which specifies a minimum volume or provision (in funding units);

(iii) colleges decide which programmes to offer but the Council has a duty to ensure sufficiency and adequacy of provision in each region;

(iv) each college's performance against its funding agreement is monitored. Growth and responsiveness is encouraged through a 'demand-led element' of funding. Underachievement can result in a reduction in funding;

(v)   the funding method gives year-on-year stability through a core allocation which in 1994/95 was 90 per cent.

4.2.3   The Method of Allocation

(i)   By expressing each college's provision in funding units, comparisons between various colleges can be made. The categories of provision and the corresponding values of units are set out in a tariff.

(ii) For 1994/95 to provide some stability of funding each college received a core funding allocation in return for a core number of units ie 90 per cent of the previous year's level in both cases.

(iii) In March each year all colleges are invited to apply for additional funding units at the standard rate of funding per unit which is set each year. In this context additional means above the core (90 per cent of the previous year level). Application can be made for further growth. The effect for most colleges of applications above the core is to drive down that college's average level of funding (frequently referred to as the ALF).

(iv) Each colleges performance against its funding agreement is monitored at times throughout the year.

4.2.4   New Concepts Introduced by Funding Method

The funding methodology supports the move to funding learning. The college's targets are set in units and the units are linked directly to funding. The unit or 'unit of activity' replaces the student FTE or weighted FTE which was the previous measure of activity used. The work which each college undertakes with each student is analyzed for funding purposes into three elements:

(i) Entry

The entry element recognizes that colleges undertake work to recruit and to counsel students which is separate from teaching them or helping them learn when they are on their learning programme. There are several entry services for students that can generate approximately 8 per cent of the units associated with a particular student. A student on a continuous programme of study can only earn entry units once even if the student attends for more than one year.

The entry element is defined as 'all the activities leading to the enrolment of a student on a learning programme'. The audit evidence in support of a claim for entry units must include a learning agreement signed on behalf of the college and by the student which includes key details of the student's planned learning. A certificate of initial guidance must also be available in respect of all students.

(ii) On Programme

The vast bulk of units in any college are earned through the On Programme element. The FEFC are progressively attaching a 'unit total' to each qualification aim and they will publish full tariff tables showing these. Other variations are also dealt with. (for example, part programmes, add-on qualifications etc) It is important to note that the unit value of a programme is independent of the time taken to deliver the programme.

There are other ways for funding units to be earned which include the following:

• If any particular student comes within the FEFC's fee remission categories and the college chooses to remit the fees for that student the college can apply for units in respect of lost income.
• If the college decides that any particular student requires additional direct learning support it can apply to the FEFC for units to meet the costs of that support. The Further

Education Funding Council will wish to establish tight guidelines as to what the different types of support should cost and what qualifies as additional support.

The on-programme element is defined as 'all activities of learning and accreditation of achievement including assessment, general and specific student support services and enrichment activities. The audit evidence in support of a claim for on-programme units must include evidence that the student was undertaking the planned learning programme in the triannual period in question and where relevant, evidence of the process leading to the accreditation of prior experience and learning.

(iii) Achievement

The final element for which units are allocated is student achievement. Units are earned if the student achieves their primary learning goal. Maximum units are gained if the achievement relates to National Training Targets. If a student achieves their primary learning goal in less than the 'usual' time the college will receive the achievement units as well as the full on programme units. If, however, a student leaves the course without completing the programme the college will lose units and not receive the achievement units.

There is a wide range of achievements listed by the FEFC which qualify. The audit evidence for achievements includes:

- listings from the awarding bodies of successful candidates;
- equivalent internal listings for certificates awarded by the colleges themselves;
- evidence of entry to a relevant programme.

4.2.5 Maximum Funding Units

In order for a college to maximize its earned funding units it should review its policies in the following areas:

- review of programmes;
- recruitment;
- retention;
- results;
- growth.

4.3 Tuition Fees

Nationally the trend is likely to be towards fee structures which more and more move toward covering the full cost of provision alongside remission policies that will attempt to ensure that no student is prevented from continuing their education because they are 'unable' to pay the tuition fee. It is important that colleges have a fee and remissions policy which they need to keep under constant review.

4.3.1 *The Policy*

A review of policy relating to the fees charged by a college of further education must take into account the requirements of the FEFC and include consideration of:

- the characteristics of the fees policy required;
- objectives;
- actual fee levels.

4.3.2 *Design Characteristics*

The desirable design characteristics of a fees policy are as follows:

(i) Clarity and Simplicity
It is important for both staff and students at the college that the fees charged are clearly communicated. The reason for the payment must be understood and the composition of a fees bill should be easy to compute. This requires a policy which is simple; the danger is that such a policy may become simplistic. Both staff and students should, however, be able to easily establish the total price associated with a programme of study.

(ii) Fair and Defensible
The policy should be seen in the eyes of a reasonable person to be fair in the sense that no particular groups are unfairly favoured or disadvantaged. Where certain groups are favoured, this happens consciously as a result of either a FEFC policy steer or in furtherance of the college's own public mission and strategic objectives and in that case is defensible.

(iii) Consistent and Coherent
The fees charged by the college and any remission granted
should be consistently applied across its programmes of study
and should, taken together, be seen to be an integrated and
logical package of charges.

(iv) Administratively Easy
The administration, implementation and management of the
fees policy should be straightforward, intelligible and easy or
else it becomes a cumbersome burden which generates inef-
ficiency, ineffectiveness, unnecessary expense and costs and
alienates the client.

(v) Competitive
The policy should place the college in a competitive position
in the local education and training market place whilst at the
same time taking cognizance of the actual (or potential)
importance of fees as a source of income for the college.

4.3.3   Objectives

The following objectives are important considerations in the formula-
tion of a fees policy. The policy should produce outcomes which:

- assist in the achievement of the college mission and strategic
  objectives particularly to increase participation;
- ensure policy and practices are legal and in particular comply
  with Consumer Protection and Credit Acts;
- place the college in an advantageous position vis a vis FEFC,
  requirements and policy steers;
- link, and be compatible, with the college's remission policy.

Finally, a major objective must be to provide a fees service to clients
which is user-friendly in the sense that it does not alienate or antago-
nize the client and, indeed, leaves the client feeling that he/she has
been dealt with by an effective and efficient consumer service.

4.3.4   Fee Levels

Decisions on fee levels and charges will need to be made under the
following headings:

    (i)   Tuition fees
- FT students 16–18;
- FT students 19 and over;
- PT students;

    (ii)   Methods of payment (for example, in advance, by instalment etc)

   (iii) Material fees and other charges
- FT students;
- PT students;

   (iv) Remission policy

    (v)   Crèche and nursery fees.

4.4 Education Contracts

Colleges receive income from various clients by whom they have been contracted to provide courses. These may include:

    (i)   LEAs for non-schedule 2 courses (mainly non-vocational adult education) and possibly some schedule 2 provision;

    (ii)   Training and Enterprise Councils;

   (iii) the HEFCE, for higher education courses run at a further education college, or direct from a higher education institution where the course is franchised to a further education college;

   (iv) other clients such as employers, health authorities and the Home Office, for example, for prison education.

4.5 Other Income

Colleges may receive grant income from a variety of sources depending on their circumstances. Such grants may include European funds.

Many colleges market specialist consultancy and research services. Income is generated from contracts entered into for such services.

Gifts and donations, often made as part of sponsorship arrangements negotiated by the college with local businesses, are an increasingly significant element within overall income. Colleges may also be in receipt of bequests from time to time and will need to be aware of any conditions attached to them.

Income may be received from student halls of residence and other student or staff accommodation provided, as well as catering facilities. The charges made are matters for the college to determine.

The use of the college's facilities when they are not required for their main purpose can be an important source of income. Some premises are particularly suitable for residential conferences and conventions, and the governing body will wish to ensure that this potential is fully exploited.

4.6 Expenditure

The College will have ensured through the planning process and the process of prioritization that all the planned activities necessary for the achievement of the objectives could be afforded. To do this the revenue and capital implications of the strategic and operational plan will have been established under the headings listed in figure 10.

- Academic staff expenditure is by far the most significant and consists of the cost of full-time and part-time academic staff required to work the hours necessary to undertake the planned activities.
- Support staff expenditure includes the costs of technicians and administrative/clerical staff. If time utilization data is maintained this will provide a basis for the allocation of this category of staff to cost centres and even to the level of programmes.
- Premises expenditure is the most significant cost after staff, the size and type of accommodation being the determining factor and the basis for apportionment to programme areas.
- Consumables/supplies and services expenditure accounts for a relatively small percentage of total recurrent costs but often occupies a significant amount of time of budget managers in monitoring and controlling their allocations. Some areas however, such as catering/refectory supplies do benefit from more detailed monitoring.

4.7 Bank Reconciliations

Due to the number of non-standard transactions processed through the college bank account, bank reconciliation may not be straightforward and the process by which a receipt is matched and recorded in the college's general ledger may be complex. Software packages are available to assist in this task and the bank itself may also assist and make its own reconciliation facility available.

EXERCISE 4: Income and Expenditure

Complete this exercise in order to establish the relative size of the items of income and expenditure of your college and their trends over a three-year period. Examine how much these have been different from the levels forecast.

1   Compare the actual and budgeted levels of income at your college over a three-year period.

Income	1993/94	1994/95	1995/96
• revenue grants from the Council			
• capital grants from the Council			
• tuition fees for further education courses			
• funding by TECs			
• contract income and tuition fees for short courses, higher education, and other directly funded provision, for example by health authorities			
• recurrent funding by the relevant Higher Education Funding Council			
• consultancy and other income from the sale of expertise and services			
• income generated by residential accommodation, catering and conferences			
• grants from the European Union and government departments			
• gifts and donations			
• farm income in agricultural colleges			
• interest earned			

2 Compare the actual and budgeted levels of expenditure at your college over a three-year period.

Expenditure	1993/94	1994/95	1995/96
• academic staff • technicians • admin and clerical • other staff • staffing • materials and equipment (books and other teaching materials, consumables, equipment and reprographics) • premises running costs (repairs and maintenance, energy, a proportion of non-domestic rates, rents, cleaning, grounds and estates, security, laundry, linen and other domestic services) • travel, subsistence and other expenses • establishment expenses (office furniture and equipment, telephones, printing, postage, insurance) • professional and agency fees (audit fee, bank charges, legal fees, payroll costs) • advertising, publicity and marketing • curriculum expenses (examination fees, external examiners' fees) • student union grant • insurance • interest payable • charges stemming from operating leases • irrecoverable value added tax			

3   On a separate sheet of paper explain any variance of over 5 per cent in any of the items of income and expenditure shown.

4   Analyse your college's recurrent funding allocation.
   (i)   Complete the following from your college's 1993/94 base

Programmes	Entry units	Entry income	On-programme units	On-programme income	Achievement units	Achievement income

   (ii)   Repeat the above for 1994/95.
   (iii)   Repeat the above for 1995/96.
   (iv)   Explain any variance of over 5 per cent in any of the figures shown from one year to the next.

5   Analyze, your college's recurrent funding allocations ordered by your college's curriculum sections.
   ie   repeat 4 above but using a department/section column rather than a programmes column

6   Investigate the effect of changing:
   (i)   student numbers;
   (ii)   each of the unit allocation variables, for example, additional support, remission, retention, etc, on your college's planned and actual unit totals and associated recurrent funding.

7   Explore the responsiveness of types of expenditure to changes in the level of activity.

8   Examine your college's fees policy:
   (i)   to what extent does it have the design characteristics covered in 4.3 of this guide;
   (ii)   to what extent does it achieve the objectives your college has set itself;
   (iii)   are the fee levels appropriate and how do they compare with the fee levels at other colleges in your area.

NOTES:

Internal Resourcing, Unit Costing, Budgeting

5.1 Introduction

The budget preparation process is driven by the objective to allocate resources at levels which are sufficient to enable the activities related to the programmes and services to be carried out at acceptable levels of quality and productivity.

The process is driven through the college's planning process and in particular through the process of academic department planning (see 5.2 below). It should seek to encourage participation by all those staff at whatever level with responsibility for managing any aspect of a budget. The process of budget building therefore, involves those staff in building up budgets within a top down framework which defines objectives, outcomes, level of activity, timescales and costs.

This section of the guide covers factors relating to internal resourcing, budgeting and the technique of unit costing all of which provides the basis by which outputs are defined and measured in terms of cost.

5.2 The Process of Academic Department Planning

The approach to strategic and operational planning invites a contribution from the college community at all levels within a central framework and involves academic departments in preparing draft departmental operating plans for the following operational year and contributing to the longer term strategic plan. In order that information is collected only once in a form which enables it to be used for different purposes, academic departments should be asked to use a standard presentation structure. The following is an example of the type of information required and an indication of the guidance given. The process starts at least one year in advance of the operational year in question and is continuous.

Information required

(a)   Longer term academic developments planned for the next five years as proposals for including in the strategic plan. Changes to the course portfolio or service offered should be clearly identified. Section 5.2.1 provides a more detailed guide.

   The deadline for completion of this should be the end of October and be produced together with a review of the previous year's operating plan.

(b)   Proposals for the academic developments which the department considers should be included in the one-year operating plan clearly indicating changes from the present year under the following headings (deadline: October) (section 5.2.2 provides a more detailed guide).
   • Courses/services which are discontinued
   • Continuing but revised course curriculum service
   • New courses

(c)   Planning for Quality — Departmental Quality Assessment Report: This is the section of the business plan which covers planning for quality. It also establishes a procedure for agreeing the targets referred to in the service level agreement. Start each section on a new page, ie:
   • Actions taken in the light of previous inspection (where relevant)
   • Aims and objectives
   • Responsiveness and range of provision
   • etc.
The start/end of each subsection should also be clearly identified and where appropriate should also start on a new page (deadline: early December).

5.2.1   Academic Developments — Strategic Plan — Guide A

The following provides an example of the possible structure and content of guides sent to curriculum managers in order to start the academic planning process and to obtain information for the college strategic plan.

Changes to Course Portfolio or Service Offered Planned in the Next Three Years

For each curriculum area/service covered by your department, please supply your judgment upon the changes you anticipate to your course portfolio or service offered over the period of the next three years. Your analysis should cover the following factors:

- changes to course provision with indicative numbers, ie, new courses starting; existing courses changing; existing courses dying;
- change of emphasis across modes of attendance;
- changes and trends in terms of level of provision; (for example, BTEC 1st, HNC)
- changes in potential for full cost activity.

For each category you should clearly state the changes you anticipate in your different market sectors and make clear all assumptions which you have made in coming to your conclusions.

Review of the Operational Plan for the Present Year

Please would you let me have the following before 17 October.

(i) An up-to-date portfolio of courses/programmes showing programme by programme for the complete year total lecturer input hours you plan to use in the present year. On the last page indicate the total for the whole department.

(ii) An updated copy of your service level agreement for the present year reflecting changes from the planned levels of activity previously agreed.

> 5.2.2 *Academic Developments — Operational Plan for Next Year — Guide B*

Current Course Portfolio or Services Offered and Developments

Curriculum Changes to the Portfolio/Services Offered

Please supply your portfolio information in terms of:

(a)   Courses/services which are discontinued:
- what are they?
- why are they being discontinued?
- what are the resource implications?

NB Do not delete these courses from the course portfolio.

(b)   Continuing but revised course curriculum/services:
- what are the courses/services being revised?
- what is the nature of the revision?
- why is the revision necessary?
- what are the resource implications?

It is accepted that revisions may take place after the deadline mentioned in this memorandum. Such revisions should be notified as they become known.

(c)   New courses/services

You will need to take into account the Further Education Funding Council desire for the further education service to grow and should list all new courses/services proposed for next year (predicted numbers of students should be as firm as possible).

- Why is the course/service proposed?
- What are the resource implications?
- Predicted student number for next year — enter on MIS Portfolio disc.

The term 'new' covers any course which:

- does not appear on the Management Information Systems current year version of your department's/unit's course portfolio; and/or
- requires approval/validation by an external validating/examining body; and/or
- is intended to be self-financing but leads to certification by a recognized examining/validation body.

All such new courses which you plan to start during the next academic year must be approved by the Academic Board.

The detail work is undertaken by the Academic Planning Subcommittee of the Academic Board.

This does not preclude short courses developing in response to the marketplace after the plan has been written. Naturally, such additional courses which are a response to the market must be flagged up in the above terms as soon as they are known.

In addition to the information required above, you will need to produce a completed course profile for all new courses which you plan for next year. Completed forms are to be received no later than October. These changes will be presented to the Academic Planning Subcommittee for approval at its November meeting.

5.2.3 Planning For Quality — Departmental Quality Assessment Report — Guide C

Your plan should demonstrate your approach to, and management of, quality. It should make explicit the ways in which the department is planning for quality by considering the following aspects of departmental provision:

- Action taken since last inspection (if applicable) or action taken in the light of the responsive college unit report
- Aims and objectives of the department
- Responsiveness and range of provision
- Governance and management
- Student recruitment, guidance and support
- Teaching and promotion of learning
- Student achievements
- Resources
- Performance indicators and targets
- Action plan for further quality improvement

Wherever possible, your planning for quality in these areas should be compatible with and reinforce the college quality planning viz:

- Student entitlement
- Monitoring and evaluation procedures
- Parents' entitlement
- Tutorial policy
- Admissions policy

In addition, you should make specific reference to the procedures you have introduced to ensure the effective induction of part-time staff as we have identified this as important to improve quality. Planning for quality and the production of the departmental quality assessment report will be an integral part of this plan. The categories listed above are taken from FEFC Circular 93/28 *Assessing Achievement* (the Circular provides a more detailed breakdown of these headings).

Your report should be the result of your inspection of your department and therefore will be evaluative rather than descriptive. It would be particularly helpful if your report adopted the format used in FEFC inspections ie for each aspect listed above identify strengths and weaknesses and describe the evidence you have used to form these judgments.

5.2.4 *Appropriate Evidence for the Departmental Quality Assessment Report*

There are many existing sources of evidence which you will be able to call upon/relate to/incorporate/append to the report to support your analysis. You may very well, of course have to codify it or restructure it to contain it within the report and within the above structure. Such evidence will include:

- programme evaluation and results summary;
- examination results;
- your direct observation (or observation of section leaders) of teaching and learning;
- your inspection of student work and discussions with students;
- your development plan and service level agreement;
- minutes and agendas of your staff, course team and management team meetings;
- your own informal PIs and monitoring procedures.

5.3 Determining the Costs of Achieving Planned Objectives — Unit Costing

Outputs are related to objectives of the college or of a department or function within the college. Unit costing enables the cost of the outputs to be measured and defines output in terms of the costs of undertaking each of the tasks which are necessary to achieve the objectives and to provide for the whole further education service by the college.

5.3.1 *Use of Unit Costing Data*

- setting targets and monitoring performance based on cost of delivery — establishing measures of efficiency;

- relating the unit of resource to the cost of delivery — measuring the relative surplus/deficit of the programme;
- identifying the marginal cost of additional students;
- evaluating alternative delivery methods;
- choosing to continue with, expand or drop programmes, courses or units.

Colleges using unit costing systems can very quickly recalculate the financial impact of change and variations in recruitment and respond accordingly.

5.3.2 College Outputs Measured as Unit Costs

These include:

- lecturer/part-time lecturer/support staff hour efficiency;
- cost per programme, course or unit;
- cost per student (programme, course or unit cost divided by enrolled students or successful students);
- cost per facility provided (lecture room, computer access, learning services, etc).

5.3.3 To Calculate Unit Costs

At the start of the budget year establish the budgeted unit costs using planned units, student numbers, planned hours loading for learning support and budgeted levels of expenditure for cost centres (staff, supplies, premises, etc). The resulting unit costs are, therefore, target figures which are available for FEFC unit applications, programme or course pricing, budget development and target setting. The calculation of actual unit costs can only be carried out at the end of the period and this provides information for internal control.

- Allocate costs as direct costs to academic and support cost centres and programmes/courses/units.
- Apportion the support centre costs to programmes/courses and academic cost centres.
- Using an absorption formula (based on lecturing staff hours) apply the absorption of academic department cost centre totals direct and apportion indirect costs to programmes or courses.

5.3.4   *The Chart of Accounts*

- Defines the basic structure of the college general ledger system and provides the basis for the preparation of college financial reports.
- Acts as a basis for financial control by setting budget targets for expense codes and reporting actual spending against budget on a code by code basis. Account codes are designed to group expenses under main and sub-codes which relate to the structure of budget responsibility. The level of detail built into each code is determined by reporting needs.

5.3.5   *The Application of Programme/Course Unit Costs*

- Establish or confirm academic and support services cost centres.
- Allocate input costs to areas of budget responsibility. Costs are allocated to expense or account codes listed in the college chart of accounts.
- Allocated costs should be direct expenditure of the cost centre account code to which they are charged, ie either academic departments support functions or programmes/courses.
- Apportion or reallocate the budgeted cost of each support cost centre between the academic cost centres using predetermined apportionment **rates**. There is no single correct method of apportioning costs to departments, programmes or courses and therefore, for administrative simplicity some measure of 'rough justice' must be accepted. In practice the apportionment base should be one that most closely reflects the linkage between the two, for example, Student Services and Learning Services could be apportioned on the basis of FEFC funding units generated by a particular department's students. Premises costs by space occupied by departments.

  The method used to apportion costs will send a message to the staff concerned about the consequence resulting from the use of staff in relation to outcomes and the use of central resources and will generate questions relating to the efficiency of the use of those resources.
- Using planned directed learning hours as an absorption rate the total cost of academic, and in some cases, support centres can be transferred to the cost unit.

  The budgeted direct cost of the academic departmental

cost centre plus the apportioned costs from support centres is divided by the programmed learning support hours for the academic year. This calculation provides an hourly learning support rate which, if applied to the programmes, courses, or units to be measured will result in the absorption of the total cost of the cost centre.

Curriculum budgets provide data on planned learning support hours. Each programme, course or module has target funding units, target student numbers, group sizes and learning support hours which determine the total aggregate learning support hours for each department.

5.3.6 Decision Making

Cost behaviour models should be developed at the level of the programme or course where it is possible to establish accurate data on break-even-levels and cost to volume to surplus/deficit patterns. Access to data which predicts how costs behave in relation to changes in activity is essential if decisions on course closure, course expansion splitting a course, increased marketing and fees policy are to be made.

A spreadsheet package can be used for most resource modelling applications to test the impact of planning assumptions relating to programme mix, growth, student numbers, planned funding units, different delivery approaches, etc.

5.4 Budgeting and Internal Resourcing

Budgeting is an organizational process covering both planning and control and an important means by which colleges can create a climate of participation particularly when the policy of maximum budget delegation is established.

5.4.1 Departmental Budgets

Departmental budgets carry responsibility for both income and expenditure and therefore, the budget outcome can be expressed in terms of a bottom line surplus or deficit (see Figure 13). The department must, therefore, budget for course and student related revenue plus other income and can apportion FEFC income using an internal formula. The

Figure 13: College departmental budgets

	Aug.	Sept.	Oct.	June	July	TOTAL
INCOME FEFC income FE tuition fees Education contracts Other income						
TOTAL INCOME						
EXPENDITURE Salary costs F/T lecturers P/T lecturers Admin staff Technicians Other						
Sub Total						
Premises costs Supplies and services Other expenditure						
TOTAL EXPENDITURE **Capital Expenditure**						
SURPLUS/DEFICIT						

most common method is to use programme groups and modes of attendance and to mirror the FEFC funding methodology for internal departmental allocations after top slicing income for central services and reserves.

If funding is attached to service level contracts funding units and students, not staff or historic allocations, then the income should be apportioned to the programme dimension of the budget matrix. This approach shows that budgeted income responsibility determined by course responsibility quantified in terms of funding units.

This approach greatly assists management planning by highlighting, in detail, where the college or department is making surpluses and incurring deficits. It also provides a mechanism for work load allocation to all staff. The resulting transparency of financial performance across a college or a department will inevitably lead to debate about the expenditure of support departments, or sections in departments with surpluses subsidizing those with deficits. Without unit costing and income apportionment at curriculum programme level, such information is not only hidden but unknown.

Once this information is made available to all staff a basis exists to develop a case for initiating curriculum changes in areas where there are significant deficit problems and in some circumstances either withdrawing course provision, increasing marketing activity, negotiating additional income to maintain a higher cost programme provision in a particular FEFC region or applying at college level an internal weighting or agreed subsidy to retain a balanced portfolio.

A budget surplus or deficit for any particular programme, when agreed, should be covered at college level and should not be carried forward by the department. Achievements by departments which are greater than those budgeted and which result in additional surpluses can be carried forward to motivate those staff concerned, particularly where additional surpluses relate to full cost work.

The use of net unit cost per FTE or the ratio of cost to funding unit total for each programme is helpful in identifying the financial implications of specific courses. Calculation of the contribution (income less variable costs) for each programme or course is another useful measure of financial viability.

Estimates of student numbers, number of funding units and other volume data sets the level of activity to be achieved and workload to be undertaken in return for the particular budget and this information will become an important part of the service level agreements at department level.

5.4.2 Budget Revision to Reflect Actual Activity

When the original budgets are prepared they are based on planned student numbers, planned funding units and other planned levels of activity, as well as planned income targets and budgeted costs.

During October once the major period of enrolment is complete, the budgets or control targets for the remainder of the college budget year should be reviewed. Where possible, actual students, income or contracted services should be substituted for the original planned figures in the budget matrix and budgeted expenditure recalculated programme by programme based on the new forecast of income and the resources needed to support the learning of students now actually enrolled.

This revision can be communicated through the issue of revised

Figure 14: Departmental budgets — based on student/funding units objective

Department	Business Studies	Engineering	Art & Design		Total
Student learning hours FT staff student contact hours PT staff student contact hours Total staff hours required Predicted FTE staff					
Academic staff cost FT staff PT staff Cost per FTE					
Support staff costs					
Total staff costs					
Premises cost per hour Supplies and services Other expenditure					
Estimated cost					
Total planned students					
Total planned funding units					

service level agreements produced with academic and support department managers.

5.4.3   The Budget Process

Budgets are allocated and expenditure monitored through budget or responsibility centres. A fully developed college budgeting system is made up of a number of interrelated budgets, which are constructed in line with the college's organizational structure, and managerial responsibilities for the provision of academic programmes, services and the achievement of specific objectives.

5.4.4   Steps in Determining a Budget

(i)   Establish planned enrolments and clearly define the specific outcomes or objectives for the budget period of each budget centre.

(ii) Define for each academic department the total student directed learning hours that different programmes will require based on planned enrolments.

(iii) Calculate the number of lecture hours required to provide the student directed learning hours.

(iv) Calculate the costs of academic staff (full-time and part-time staff) required by each department associated with the total enrolments and total learning hours.

(v) Calculate the cost per lecturer hour at departmental level (full-time and part-time staff).

(vi) Calculate support staff costs and supplies and services costs required by each department to deliver the programme and provide the services.

(vii) Distribute lecturer costs as a cost per hour to programmes, courses, and modules. Distribute academic department direct costs based on identified need.

(viii) Total costs for each programme and department to establish the budgeted cost of the college's total academic programme.

5.5 Service Level Agreements

The Service Level Agreement is an 'internal contract' linking the budgets to the planned level of activity and the achievement of planned objectives.

The following provides an example of the possible structure and content of a service level agreement although each college may wish to adapt this for their use.

Example of Service Level Agreement

Department of _____

1   Introduction
Budgets are delegated as part of a service level agreement. The department/unit receives a budget in exchange for:
(a)   delivering its course portfolio;
(b)   undertaking agreed developments shown in the strategic plan;
(c)   providing a specific level of servicing to other departments/ units;
(d)   meeting specific targets which include:
- effectiveness/quality targets;
- recruitment levels;
- target income.

2   Course portfolio
The department's current course portfolio should be obtained from Management Information Services by the Head of Department, checked for accuracy by the Head and a signed dated copy sent to the Vice Principal by the end of June.

The departments planned total programme hours for the academic year is:
(a)   FE Funding Council programmes ...... hours
(b)   Income bearing programmes ...... hours
Total

3   Undertaking agreed developments
A summary of new developments planned within the year should be sent to the Vice Principal by the end of June. These details will then become part of the service level agreement.

Tasks to be carried out by staff in the department which are necessary to achieve each target should be listed in an action plan which should be sent to the Vice Principal no later than the end of July.

4   Inwards and outwards servicing
Full details of the planned service provided:
(a)   by the department for other departments (including secondments);
(b)   by other departments for your department;
should be sent to the Vice Principal by the end of June.

5   Effectiveness/quality targets

A summary of these should be agreed with the Vice Principal and details sent to him by the end of June.

6   Recruitment levels

Using the actual student target enrolments for each programme/ course shown on the portfolio of courses convert the enrolments to funding units to show a detailed build up of the departments overall recruitment target.

The course by course breakdown should be returned to the Vice Principal by the end of September.

7   Target income

The income target figures have been calculated based on historic information and current inflation levels but you may wish to suggest a higher or lower figure based on your knowledge of the current market. In that case the following year's budget figures will be altered in proportion to your adjusted figure. This will be done in consultation with you.

(a)   Estimated FEFC income

(b)   FE tuition fee income

(c)   Education contract income

(d)   Other income

(e)   Total estimated income

Note   A spreadsheet showing the breakdown of tuition fees for each programme, course and/or module/unit is available from the Finance Office. Heads of Department should ensure that the spreadsheet for their department is kept up to date and is accurate. A signed and dated copy should be sent by the Head of Department to the Vice Principal by the end of July.

8   Full-time staff budget

The department's list of established full-time staff has been checked and agreed.

(a)   Full-time lecturers

(b)   Administrative and clerical staff

(c)   Technician and other staff

(d)   Total full-time staffing budget

Your full-time staff budget has been set based on the department's agreed establishment. In the event of the actual expenditure on basic salaries for these staff being higher or lower the budget will be adjusted. Control of full-time staff expenditure is achieved through control of the agreed establishment lists.

9   Part-time staff budgets

Efficient use of full-time staff, total contact hours and programme hours used will enable the number of part-time hourly contracts to be set at a level which will allow virement from the total staffing budgets shown into the consumable/equipment budget. Heads of Department should provide the Vice Principal with a detailed plan of the number/cost of part-time contract hours that they intend to use from 1 August to the following July.

(a)   Part-time lecturer budget
(b)   Part-time lecturer hours (planned)
        (to be completed by Head of Department)
(c)   Administrative/clerical/technical staff overtime budget

10   Capitation/consumable budget

Virement from the staff budget will be possible after agreement with the Vice Principal when efficiency savings are made.

A maximum of one-third of the above allocation should be spent each term without prior agreement from the Vice Principal.

11   Capital expenditure budget

12   Growth and development plan expenditure

Normal order books should **not** be used to spend this allocation. A separate order book must be used in liaison with the Financial Services.

13   Assets Register

The Head of Department should ensure that the Assets Register for their department is accurate/up to date and carry out the necessary checks of the assets shown.

A signed and dated copy should be sent to the Vice Principal at the end of each term by the Head of Department confirming this and drawing any irregularities to his attention. The first copy should be sent at the end of June.

The following diagram illustrates the interface between the strategic plan, departmental academic plans and the production of internal service level contracts.

Figure 15:   *Internal resourcing — producing the internal service level contract*

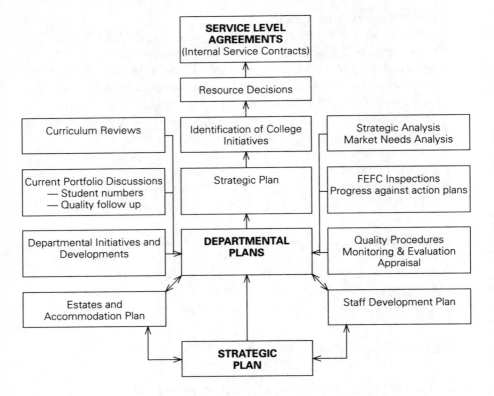

EXERCISE 5: Internal Resource Allocation —
Unit Costing — Budgeting

Explore and consider the information base and mechanisms for internal resource allocation at your College by completing this exercise.

1 Sources of income
  (a) Indicate below the major sources of college income by type and proportion.

	Type	£	Proportion
(i)	FEFC recurrent grant	....	.... (70%)
(ii)	FEFC capital allocation	....	....
(iii)	Income from TEC	....	....
(iv)	Contract income	....	....
(v)	Tuition fees	....	....
(vi)	....	....	....
(vii)	....	....	....
(viii)	....	....	....
(ix)	....	....	....
(x)	....	....	....

  (b) Using the above totals draw up a table to the sub-group or departmental level of Income

Department	i	ii	iii	iv	viii	ix	x	Total	% of College Total
Business studies									
Engineering									

2 Uses of Income (Expenditure)
  (a) Indicate below the major items of College expenditure by type and proportion

	Type	£	Proportion
(i)	Lecturing staff full-time	....	.... (70%)
(ii)	Lecturing staff part-time	....	....
(iii)	....	....	....
(iv)	....	....	....
(v)	....	....	....
(vi)	....	....	....
(vii)	....	....	....
(viii)	....	....	....
(ix)	....	....	....
(x)	....	....	....

(b) Using the above totals draw up a table to the sub-group or departmental level

Department	i	ii	iii	iv	viii	ix	x	Total	% of College Total
Business studies									
Engineering									

3 Staffing Expenditure
   (a) Prepare a table showing staffing costs for your college. This should include contingency allowances, for example, cover for staff development, cover for paid absence (sickness, maternity leave).

	Type of staff	Number of people	FTE number	Average salary	Total cost
i	Central management				
ii	Management spine				
iii					
iv					
v	Lecturer Part-time lecturer				
vi	Technicians				
vii	Administration				
viii					
ix					
x	Cover Paid absence Staff development				
	TOTALS				

(b) Using the above total costs draw up a table to the sub-group or departmental level as in 1(b) and 2(b) above.

4 Explore the budget setting process
   List the strengths and weaknesses of the following two methods used for determining internal budgets and resource requirements:
   (a) using a formula approach which passes on income directly to the section or department within the college that earns it and which allocates all types of income and expenditure specifically to that department (cash budgeting);
   (b) using the strategic and operational planning process and the measurement of changes in the cost of departments' outputs from the previous year which are planned to change the budget from the previous year's level (commitment budgeting).

5 Using the information contained in section 5.5 of this guide produce a 'Service Level Agreement' or internal contract in respect of one:
   (a) academic department;
   (b) academic support department (for example, Student Services);
   (c) administration services department (for example, Financial Services).

NOTES:

Performance Measurement and Monitoring

6.1 Introduction

Performance measurement indicators are one of a number of guides that can be used by the college to take action to remedy any problems and weaknesses that may be identified. The decision as to what indicators to use is not a simple one for there can be conflicts between efficiency and effectiveness measures as well as between the College's and students' perceptions of each. The different perceptions of what is most important should be considered when decisions are made on appropriate actions to be taken. It is vital to remember that the production of the indicators is not 'action'. It is the use to which the indicators are put that is important.

6.2 Performance Indicators are Set Within Three Measurement Areas

6.2.1 *Effectiveness — The Relationship of Outputs to College Objectives*

This is the most difficult area to ensure coverage as objectives are often qualitative in nature 'achievement of student success' or the provision of a 'stimulating learning environment'. Performance indicators can, however, act as a guide to effectiveness by, for example, tracking performance in relation to successful course completion, growth in students using the service or age mix of students attending learning programmes.

6.2.2 *Efficiency — The Conversion of Inputs to Outputs*

Efficiency based indicators track the performance of activities through indicators such as the average level of funding and the units costs per course/student.

6.2.3   Economy

The conversion of allocated resources, usually expressed in financial terms, to resource inputs, such as full-time staff, part-time staff, support staff, supplies of materials and equipment and space. Indicators in this area can track the performance activities such as the mix of and relative cost of different categories of staff, maintenance and buildings, purchasing, etc.

Each of the three performance measurement areas outlined above can be further sub-divided into quantitative (valued added) indicators or qualitative (management process). The diagram, Figure 16, indicates specific indicators under each heading.

Figure 16:   Effectiveness — efficiency — economy performance indicators

Indicators	Effectiveness	Efficiency	Economy
Quantitative (value-added)	• student number growth rate • retention/continuation rate to qualifications • achievement rate • positive destination rate • recruitment profile related to catchment profile	• cost per student • cost per successful student • ratio of staff costs to student costs	• Value for FEFC unit • ratio of FEFC money to other sources
Qualitative (management process)	• amount of flexible learning on offer • availability of guidance • availability of learning support • number of satisfied customers • profile amongst public • valued added through the learning process	• room utilization rate • % staff on flexible contracts • number of learning centres/ flexible learning arrangements • investments in learning technology • cost per unit of value-added	• % reduction in purchasing costs • amount of full cost recovery work #

Standing advisory group on value for money and value-added
Valuing Further Education:
A position paper on Value for Money and Value-Added

6.3 Further Education Funding Council Performance Indicators

6.3.1 The FEFC identifies three main purposes of College performance indicators:

- to enable colleges and the Council to monitor the changes in performance at each institution over a period of time;
- to enable colleges to assess their achievements relative to comparable institutions;
- to provide information for the DFE, training and enterprise councils (TECs), the Council and the general public as part of the accountability for spending public funds.

Three criteria which performance indicators should satisfy if they are to work are identified as:

- they need to be clearly designed so that a proper comparison is possible;
- they should be collected as part of other activities;
- they should be seen as relating to key areas of activity in colleges.

6.3.2 The FEFC has a duty to ensure that there are satisfactory arrangements for assessing the quality of provision in the further education sector. It discharges its duty through its inspectorate who assess and make judgments on the balance between strengths and weaknesses of each aspect of the work of the college that they inspect which includes:

- responsiveness and range of provision;
- governance and management;
- student recruitment guidance and support;
- resources: staffing, equipment/learning resources, accommodation;
- curriculum areas;
- teaching and the promotion of learning;

- student achievements;
- quality assurance.

The inspectors use a five point scale to record their judgments:

- grade 1 — provision which has many strengths and very few weaknesses;
- grade 2 — provision in which the strengths clearly outweigh the weaknesses;
- grade 3 — provision with a balance of strengths and weaknesses;
- grade 4 — provision in which the weaknesses clearly outweigh the strengths;
- grade 5 — provision which has many weaknesses and very few strengths.

6.3.3   *The FEFC collect performance indicators from college statistical returns which include:*

- PI 1 — Achievement of Funding Target — an indicator of college effectiveness
- PI 2 — Student Enrolment Trends — an indicator of colleges responsiveness
- PI 3 — Student Continuation — an indicator of programme effectiveness
- PI 4 — Learning Goals and Qualifications — an indicator of student achievements
- PI 5 — Attainment of NVQ or Equivalent — an indicator of contribution to national targets
- PI 6 — Average Levels of Funding — an indicator of value for money.

6.3.4   *The continuing development of performance indicators which measure the value added by colleges to a student's performance is likely to be given an increasingly high priority and the results linked to the allocation by the FEFC of College's Recurrent Funding.*

6.3.5   *Figure 17 indicates performance indicators derived from objectives and planned achievements detailed in college's strategic
and operational plans. On one axis of the matrix planned
objectives such as:*

- increased student achievement;
- increasing student numbers/achieving enrolment targets;
- improving efficiency;
- improving value for money;

are linked through the other axis of the diagram to:

- national targets;
- the funding methodology.

The result is the performance indicators shown in the bottom section
of the diagram.

6.3.6   *Figure 18 shows the relation between the decision on what
indicators to use and the college's internal resource allocation
mechanisms linking resource input with planned outcomes and
the achievement of objectives shown in the college's strategic
and operational plans.*

6.3.7   *Figure 19 recognizes the College's need to establish other internal indicators at a more detailed level which relate directly to
that college's business plan or which it may wish to keep con-
fidential for business reasons. These indicators can also address
areas which the college has found are particularly important to
its local community, its students and other customers. The college can also address any conflicts between efficiency and effectiveness measures and informal strategic decisions relating to
efficiency targets, for example, a college's published average
level of funding is a measure of overall output against overall
recurrent grant input and the difference between this and the
college's internal operational average level of funding provides
the college with a mechanism to allocate resources for developments, manage risk and generate reserves.*

Figure 17: Performance indicators I

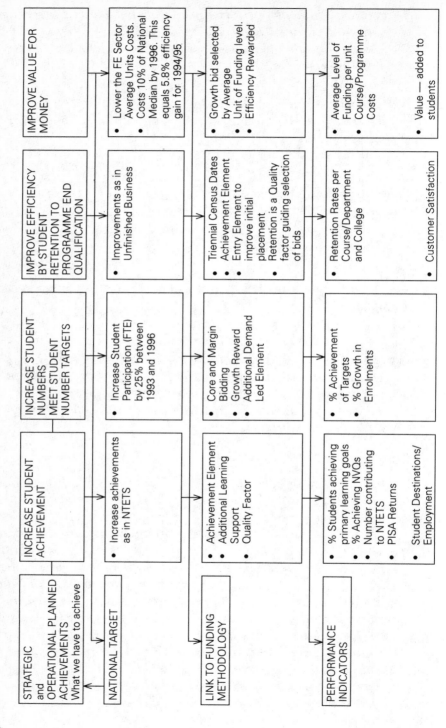

	INCREASE STUDENT ACHIEVEMENT	INCREASE STUDENT NUMBERS MEET STUDENT NUMBER TARGETS	IMPROVE EFFICIENCY BY STUDENT RETENTION TO PROGRAMME END QUALIFICATION	IMPROVE VALUE FOR MONEY
STRATEGIC and OPERATIONAL PLANNED ACHIEVEMENTS What we have to achieve				
NATIONAL TARGET	• Increase achievements as in NTETS	• Increase Student Participation (FTE) by 25% between 1993 and 1996	• Improvements as in Unfinished Business	• Lower the FE Sector Average Units Costs. Costs 10% of National Median by 1996. This equals 5.8% efficiency gain for 1994/95
LINK TO FUNDING METHODOLOGY	• Achievement Element • Additional Learning • Support • Quality Factor	• Core and Margin Bidding • Growth Reward • Additional Demand Led Element	• Triennial Census Dates • Achievement Element • Entry Element to improve initial placement • Retention is a Quality factor guiding selection of bids	• Growth bid selected by Average • Unit of Funding level. • Efficiency Rewarded
PERFORMANCE INDICATORS	• % Students achieving primary learning goals • % Achieving NVQs • Number contributing to NTETS • PISA Returns • Student Destinations/ Employment	• % Achievement of Targets • % Growth in Enrolments	• Retention Rates per Course/Department and College • Customer Satisfaction	• Average Level of Funding per unit • Course/Programme Costs • Value — added to students

Figure 18: Performance indicators II

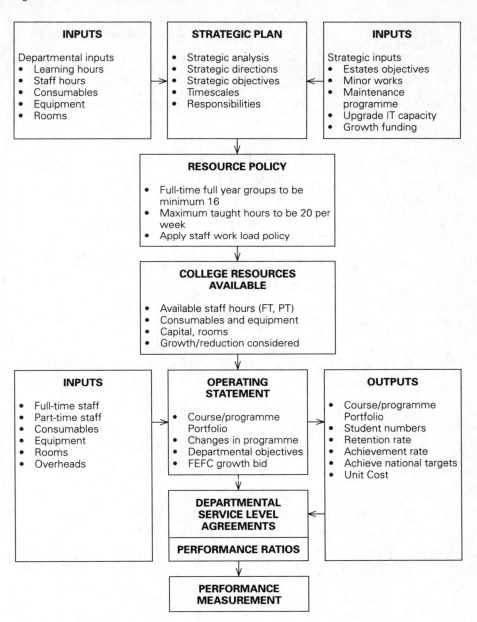

Figure 19: *College specific indicators of performance*

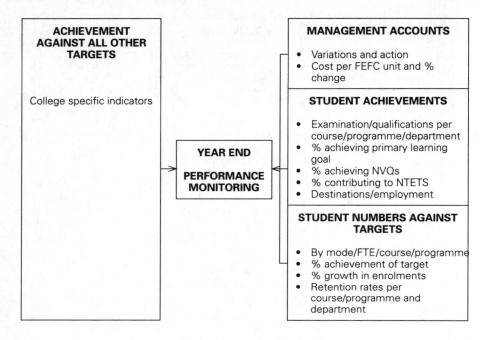

6.4 Comparisons of Actual Performance Against the Budget

6.4.1 Management Systems

In order to become more business-like, colleges have developed the following systems:

- a planning system which matches the resources received from all sources with the programmes the college has to deliver. This system establishes targets for individual sections and managers;
- a control system to ensure the expenditure plans are being met, income and recruitment targets are being achieved and quality maintained;
- a management information system which informs all concerned about planned and actual performance and supports both processes.

Most colleges have made significant investment in specialist computerized management information systems designed to serve these functions.

6.4.2   Comparisons of Actual Performance Against the Budget — Budget Monitoring

Each college requires a process which systematically compares actual performance against the budget and communicates this information in good time to the heads of responsibility centres.

All colleges should be operating comprehensive, integrated computerized management information systems which are able to cater for this. Colleges need to maintain sufficient accounting records to construct income and expenditure statements for budgetary control and for their 'income-generating' activities.

The computer system needs to define all income and expenditure closely using identification codes and sub-codes. This enables every element of income or expenditure to be located to the correct department/unit (cost centre) on a day-to-day basis. Budget monitoring statements can then be prepared to the detail required. These may include:

- a college income and expenditure statement showing spent and committed figures against each expenditure head compared with the budget available — the percentage of the budget spent against the percentage of the budgetary period completed can also be shown;
- a specific departmental income and expenditure statement showing the above information for each cost centre;
- a specific list of actual purchases for each cost centre and for each budget heading.

6.4.3   College Level Monitoring Statements

Income and expenditure monitoring statements can be produced at college level that are similar to the specimen statements shown at 6.4.4. The following charts show a specimen:

- profiled budgeted cash flow monitoring statement;
- balance sheet monthly monitoring statement.

Figure 20:   Budgeted cash flow projection

	Aug.	Sept.	Oct.	Nov.	Etc.	**Tot.**
Receipts						
FEFC recurrent grant						
Other FEFC grants						
TEC income						
Invoiced income						
Cash income						
Bank interest						
Other						
Total receipts						
Payments						
Payroll						
Trade purchases						
Contractual payments						
Capital expenditure						
Other expenditure						
Transf.to/from short term dep.						
Total Payments						
Net payments/receipts						
Opening cash balance						
Closing cash balance						

Figure 21: Balance sheet

	This Month	Budget	Last Month	Position at date previous year
Fixed Assets				
1010 Land and buildings at valuation				
1020 Equipment and vehicles at cost				
1050				
1110 Depreciation on property				
1120 Depreciation on equipment and vehicles				
1150				
1200 Net value of fixed assets				
Current Assets				
1210 Stocks				
1220 Debtors				
1230 Cash at bank and on hand				
1240 Short-term deposit				
Current Liabilities				
1300 Creditors				
1310 Tax and pension contributions				
1320 Payments on account				
1400 Provisions				
1500				
1610 Capital Reserve				
1620 Restricted Reserve				
Income & Expenditure Account				
1730 Brought forward				
1740 First 4 months				
1750 Current Year — per I & E				
1760 Current Year — transfer from reser.				
1800				

6.4.4   Departmental Monitoring Statements

Figure 22:   Budget monitoring statement

Department/College ....

	Current Month Position			Year to Date Position				
% Year to Date ____ Accounting Period ____	Budget Month	Actual Month	Variance Month	Total Budget	Actual to Date	% to Date	Budget Balance	Previous years total at same date
Income FEFC income FEFC tuition fees Education contracts Other income Total income								
Expenditure FT lecturers PT lecturers Admin staff Technician staff Other staff Total staff								
Premises costs Supplies and services Other expenditure								
Total expenditure								
Capital expenditure								
Surplus/deficit								

6.4.5   Monitoring Information — for Governors

Governors require regular up to date summary information so that they can ensure that they are meeting their financial responsibilities, be confident in the financial management of the college and that financial risk is minimised. The following information presented monthly under the heading 'Financial Report and Indicators' is easy to read, understand and explain.

Example of Financial Report And Indicators

1   *Student Numbers*
    By the end of the spring term _____ students had been enrolled
    to date this academic year.
    (a) It is likely that the college will meet its student target.
    (b) Growth in weighted FTE students attending FEFC programmes
         is _____
    (c) Growth as measured in funding units will be calculated at the
         end of the summer term.

2   *Income Generation*
    Overall income generation at _____ is better than planned (up
    approximately £200,000 at date).

3   *Overall Expenditure*
    Total expenditure is _____ and the percentage spent at _____ against
    the percentage of the financial year gone which is within budget.

4   *Staffing Expenditure*
    Overall staffing expenditure at _____ has a favourable variance
    year to date of approximately _____

5   *Debtors*
    Over 2000 invoices have been issued and 800 customer accounts
    opened during the past year. They represent a value of over _____.
    In January _____ invoices issued were _____ and in February _____.
         At the end of March debtors due on 28 February _____ stood
    at of which _____ (79 per cent) belonged to fifteen organisations.
    In March _____ cash was collected.

6   *Student drop out rates (demand led element)*
    At the end of April the college will receive _____ demand led
    element ie _____ more than the planned _____. (Governors
    will recall that in December the college received _____ less than
    planned.)

7   *Cash Position*
    On the 18 March the college's cash balance stood at _____.

8   *Funding Bid to the FEFC*
    The college's bid for funding to the FEFC in respect of _____ has
    been sent.

6.5 Individual Student Records, Learning Agreements, Certificate of Initial Assessment and Guidance

6.5.1 Funding

The Funding Council funds the College according to work done with the student in three stages — entry, on programme and achievement. The first stage 'entry' involves initial advice and guidance offered to students before and during enrolment and during induction. The evidence that the work has been done is contained in individual student records, learning agreements, other information relating to the student and a certificate of initial assessment and guidance.

6.5.2 Student Records

The college has to make available for the FEFC audit an individual record of each student's personal details, primary learning goal and programme. This individualized student record (ISR) enables the FEFC to calculate the level of activity in the college for funding purposes at three points every year. These census points are in November, February and May.

6.5.3 Audit

The FEFC also requires the college to prove that it is providing what it says it is by requiring documents to be signed by staff and all FEFC funded full- and part-time students such as those specified below.

6.5.4 Learning Agreement

The Learning Agreement states, among other things, the student's primary learning goal. The primary learning goal is the FEFC fundable qualification aim or aims, or other equivalent objectives to be achieved by the student within a minimum period of twelve months. It excludes qualifications which are either subsidiary or equivalent to other qualifications in the same subject already included in the primary learning goal.

This enables the college to see the extent to which primary learning goals have been met at any time during the individual student's learning programme.

6.5.5 *Certificate of Initial Assessment and Guidance*

The Certificate of Initial Assessment and Guidance confirms that the student has received satisfactory initial guidance and support from the college staff.

The college will rely for a large part of its funding on reliable information on what students are doing and have done, backed up by documentary evidence. The FEFC will be able to check this simply by comparing the ISRs of a sample of students with the documentary evidence held by the college in the form of learning contracts, Certificates of Initial Assessment and Guidance and qualification lists.

6.5.6 *Further Information*

FEFC Circular 93/39: *Recurrent Funding for 1994–5*
FEFC Circular 94/10: *ISR Data Collection 1994–5*
FEFC Circular 94/23: *Modified Audit Evidence for Entry Unit 1994–5*

6.6 Preparation of the College's Period End Report and Accounts

The financial memorandum between the FEFC and the college states that the college shall provide the council with audited accounts for the financial year, signed by the Principal and Chairman of the Governors, no later than the end of November each year. Closedown of ledgers, preparation of financial accounts and the timing of the audit fieldwork need to be planned, taking into account the cycle of meetings necessary and the timelag required between each, to prepare and circulate papers to committees of the college's governing body which will review the work done. Although the closedown of ledgers, preparation of final accounts and working papers ready for audit is likely to start in earnest on 1 August each year, many tasks can be carried out before that time.

Annex A provides an example of a college's end of period accounts.

6.6.1 *Working Papers Required for Audit*

- Draft report and financial statements:
  Report by the Board of Governors or equivalent

Income and expenditure account
Statement of total recognized gains and losses
Statement of historical cost surpluses and deficits
Balance sheet
Cash flow statement
Notes of the financial statements, including accounting policies

- Copies of original and revised budgets and outrun for the year, with brief explanations for all significant over/under spends against budget. (A copy of any management information prepared for senior management and/or the Finance Committee should be adequate.)
- A copy of the trial balance at 31 July, plus purchase and sales ledgers.
- Working papers showing the aggregation of account codes from the trial balance to the income and expenditure account and balance sheet.
- Reconciliations of all control accounts, including salaries and season ticket loan control accounts, VAT control account, sales ledger and purchase ledger and cash control accounts.
- Analyses of any suspense accounts.
- If applicable, working papers showing the consolidations of the college and its subsidiaries.
- Copies of guidance notes issued to departments detailing closedown procedures, with specific reference to the preparations of accruals listings, sundry debtors listings and requirements for stock taking (if applicable).
- Correspondence with the local authority confirming the agreement of balances transferred and giving details of any matters not yet resolved.

EXERCISE 6: Performance Measurement and Monitoring

This exercise will help the user of this guide consider the best strategy for measuring performance and monitoring the implementation of the strategic and operational plan, ie how, when and by whom.

1   How will the implementation of the plan be monitored. Describe the role of:
   (a)   governors
   (b)   central management
   (c)   senior managers/heads of department/budget managers
   (d)   other

2   Check that appropriate targets for progress have been set against each of the objectives in the plan:
   (a)   clearly defined performance indicators (key success factors)
   (b)   indication of timing and cost
   (c)   clearly defined responsibilities

3   What information will be needed to monitor and evaluate progress towards the achievement of objectives and targets set in the plan?

4   Who is responsible for ensuring appropriate corrective action is taken if necessary if problems are identified:
   (a)   timing (lack of progress)
   (b)   costs
   (c)   changed circumstances

5   Using the four diagrams relating to performance indicators, figures 13–16, insert targets against or levels against each item using last year's actuals. Repeat for the current year.

6   Using the six FEFC performance indicators prepare a spreadsheet on which last year's actual levels should be input and the present year's targets.

7   Regular financial reporting routines designed to produce summary management information are essential so that managers can review this and take appropriate follow up action, if any control breakdowns or possible material mis-statements are identified.

(a)   Describe briefly in respect of your college how management ensure that all fee and other financial activity is reflected in the financial statements.

....

....

....

....

....

....

(b)   To what extent is an accruals basis adopted in regular financial reports.

....

....

....

....

....

....

....

....

8   Briefly describe the main features of your college's plan for the implementation of individual student records. Highlight five problems identified and briefly indicate how these were overcome.

....

....

....

....

....

NOTES:

Improving Efficiency and Increasing Income

7.1 Introduction

If a college is to take advantage of new opportunities, some spending will have to cease and/or productivity will have to rise in order to release resources. It should be remembered that a more effective return, or growth, in what is provided for the same level of cost has a similar effect over a period of time to a reduction in overall cost.

Colleges need to be developing a range of responses to efficiency improvements. This will involve the questioning of current patterns of resource input and deployment and knowing clearly what the present position is when compared with the college's resource objectives. It is necessary to question the primary purpose of each task or reason for expenditure and link efficiency savings to impact and contribution to the achievement of the college's objectives and to the future role of the college.

Clearly, spending less or doing more with the same has to be addressed with sensitivity and shown to all to be a means to an end rather than the end itself. Responding to the challenges of efficiency improvement and introducing new methods of resource deployment can be regarded as negative or it can be a catalyst for creativity. Everyone within the college community must understand that the actions are being taken to enhance the achievement of the college's shared objectives and that the college is not losing sight of its primary function to provide a high quality further education service. Income generation has a part to play in generating development income and the level of reserves, particularly in the short term, but care has to be taken that the bottom line profit shown is not illusory.

7.2 Management of Staffing Expenditure

7.2.1 *Any serious study of cost reduction options has to address expenditure on staffing as it represents approximately three-quarters of the college's recurrent cost. This is the main focus of attention when seeking to reduce the average level of funding and the improvement of staff efficiency. Factors which need to be considered include:*

(a)   increasing the number of hours for which staff are available;
(b)   reducing the number of student learning hours for which a direct lecturer input is required;
(c)   increase the average group size or throughput of students per lecturer hour;
(d)   growth in students achieving their primary learning goal per lecturer supported learning hour.

Cost reduction options also include:

(a)   introduction of the 'workload' approach to the allocation of duties for all staff clearly linked to outcomes and a common unit of activity;
(b)   introduction of a rank order for programmes in terms of entry units, on programme units, achievement units and total units earned with a view to alternative modes of delivery/learning support or possible closure/expansion of options;
(c)   ranking programmes in terms of learning support hours allocated and dividing input hours into (b) above to create a ratio of units earned per hour;
(d)   establishing/increasing the profitability of full cost courses. It is necessary to question whether it is desirable to continue to run high cost programmes or low fixed income activities. It may be possible to negotiate additional financial assistance if this is necessary so that a particular area of work or service can continue in a particular region of the country;
(e)   Strategic priorities reflect a choice from a range of possible objectives based on information from the strategic analysis including the total financial and human resources available. The skills and capabilities of staff are a key factor in shaping priorities and, therefore, the college's ability to achieve its mission. The college plan must indicate how human resources relate to the delivery of the college's objectives including:

  •   the planning process for developing the College's strategy and ensuring matching staff resources are available;
  •   the mechanisms for tackling any mismatch of skills needed

for delivery of the strategic objectives and how the College's priorities are balanced with individuals needs for (re)training and development;

- the staff development process — a separate staff development plan should be available which meets the staff development needs of the corporation as reflected in the strategic plan and the needs of the individual members of staff;
- the employment and recruitment policy.

The staff planning framework has the following components which reflect the needs identified in departmental plans as well as in the college strategic and operational plan.

(a) the identification of resources; (staff numbers, contractual terms and flexibility of deployment, skills, experience and qualifications, commitment, enthusiasm and innovative energy);

(b) matching existing resources to curriculum and business plans;

(c) identifying current gaps in resources;

(d) predicting in the light of curriculum plans, future shortages and areas of over-resourcing;

(e) agreeing the balance required between staff resources needed to deliver the service and those needed to support the delivery processes;

(f) determining a schedule and budget requirements for bringing staff resources into line with curriculum and business plans.

These components can be dealt with operationally through departmental service level agreements, which link resourcing to the achievement of the planned objectives.

7.2.2 *The strategic plan also includes a statement on the following management issues:*

(a) institutional ethos;

(b) equality of opportunity;

(c) employment and recruitment policies and procedures;

(d) balancing the acquisition of new resources with the development and the redeployment of existing ones;

(e) communication of policies and procedures of staff;

(f) employee relations;

(g) performance review;

(h) health, safety and welfare policies and practices.

The personnel plan should provide full details of the above issues and will also:

- indicate the programme hours used for all courses by departments;
- indicate the college's staffing establishment;
- indicate a separate analysis of part-time staff hours/costs.

7.3 Management of Capital Assets to Reduce Costs

The next highest area of expenditure after staff costs relates to the college grounds and buildings (capital assets). The first steps in reducing cost in this area requires the establishment of an accurate database drawn from an audit of facilities using FEFC space norms and a clear relationship between the way the resource is managed, defining responsibilities and accountability. The resource levels needed by the educational programmes, including the space they require can be determined and allocated alongside the associated budgetary provision. Factors which can be explored and which will generate cost reductions include:

- central allocation of rooms and the use of computerized timetabling;
- introduction of cost centre management of rooms with reward mechanisms and sanctions;
- analysis of room utilization factors (usage × occupancy) and rank order the findings, review lower quartile results and reallocate/change use of space;
- ensuring need matches size of room (rank occupancy);
- extending concept of room availability across full year, full working week and full working day (mode free flexible use).

7.4 Non-staff Recurrent Expenditure

The number of areas in the non-staff recurrent expenditure category is large but possible savings may only be one-off savings. Economies possible tend to give small returns and they are often only partial in their coverage. On the negative side, in considering savings in this area of expenditure there is also the danger that cuts can impact directly and immediately on the level and quality of the service.While the following areas should be carefully considered, in terms of value for money, the fact that the examples listed are clear, simple to understand and comparatively easy to tackle, should not make them the main focus when looking for efficiency savings. However, these areas should be reviewed:

- catering services (perhaps considering executive leasing);
- professional services (review of the cost of any 'extras' associated with additional services provided by contracted services, for example, bank, auditors, payroll, etc);
- purchasing (see section 3.2);
- marketing and publicity;
- finance and contract management;
- utilities;
- security;
- examinations and validation;
- staff development;
- expenses and hospitality.

7.5   How Can Colleges Increase Their Income?

If colleges increase their income they are free to spend it as the governors decide. For many colleges increasing earned income is a strategic objective. This section of the guide covers ways in which this can be done.

7.5.1   *Most colleges receive the majority of their income from the Further Education Funding Council (see section 4.2). Policies and procedures bearing on the following will help an individual college maximize this source of income:*

- review of its programmes;
- growth strategy;
- recruitment policy;
- retention of students;
- achievement of results by students.

7.5.2   *Colleges can act to increase their development income by:*

- increasing their efficiency and effectiveness;
- boosting the sales of services to clients who are prepared to pay the full cost of provision;
- improving their marketing.

7.5.3 *Examples of services offered at full cost by many colleges include:*

- short courses designed to meet particular industrial needs;
- consultancy for individual companies or trade groups;
- the provision of specialist testing services using college's equipment when not used for teaching;
- the provision of self-study packs or open learning materials to support a company's own training programme.

7.5.4 *Other ways in which a college can increase its income include:*

- promoting the use of college buildings or lettings — particularly if the college has a town centre site;
- maximizing income from the sale of goods and services provided during practical teaching sessions (for example, hairdressing, catering, horticulture);
- the sale of advertising space in college publicity material.

7.5.5 *There is a number of organizational structures through which full cost or self-financing services can be offered. A college can use one or more than one of these if it wishes:*

(a) establish a separate college company through which all full cost work or commercial activities are offered. This option requires both legal and financial advice (see section 7.5.3);

(b) establish a separate college unit which, while still part of the departmental structure of the college, would have its own staff, exclusive use of its own accommodation and other resources. The Director of the Unit would be responsible for producing and agreeing plans, volume of activity, budgets and income/expenditure targets. Any use of other college staff and accommodation would be on separate and specific contracts;

(c) require all departments in the college to plan for enterprise activity. Departments would be responsible for identifying and marketing the work they might do and carrying out the work within the department. Target income/expenditure would be agreed as part of the normal operational planning process and any additional surplus would be retained by the department;

(d) establish a central coordinating section as part of the marketing function within the college with responsibility for advising on all full cost work or commercial activity, act as a single point of contact for potential customers and monitor quality across the college.

Whatever, the arrangement or mix of arrangements there are certain requirements of enterprise units for the promotion of enterprise services that are common to all. These are shown in the diagram below (figure 23).

Figure 23: Requirements of enterprise units

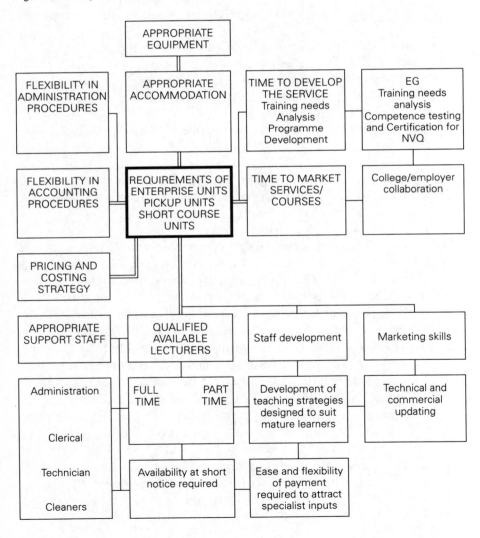

7.5.3   *One particular area where difficulties could arise would be in any trading activities carried on by the college. The College's exemption from income tax or corporation tax might not cover these activities and the activities could also give rise to VAT. In addition, business rate relief could be challenged. If income trading activities is contemplated, legal advice and/or advice from the Charity Commissioners, as appropriate, should be sought.*

7.5.4   *Ideally the college should have a series of standard contracts for the various types of services it offers, and these should clearly state the legal position of the contract, the financial arrangements and the VAT position, as well as details which spell out the main points of the contract itself. This ensures that the financial position of the college is properly safeguarded and that any new contract signed on behalf of the college fits into the college strategy and is properly drawn up. Contract review mechanisms, including legal advice, must be in place to ensure that standard contracts of outside bodies in respect of new business are satisfactory.*

7.6   Pricing

If a course is to be fully self-financing then it is necessary to ensure that the prices charged are at least sufficient to cover the full cost, including overheads, of the service provided.

As far as possible the price will be the maximum the market will bear. When following this strategy most colleges will ensure that their full cost programmes reinforce the overall further education service provided by the college and are not promoted at the expense of other provisions. The strategy for pricing may be based on a balancing policy of maximizing total income, maximizing the volume of programmes run and ensuring that total expenditure for this type of programme is contained within the income earned.

7.7 Course Costing

An Example of a Course Costing Form

A Department .... Financial Year .... Form No ......
Course/programme/service Title .... MIS Code ....
Company name and address..
....
Contact name......................... Telephone no.............. Fax ....
Total directed hours............................ Price per hour ....
Group fee................................. Fee per student...........................
Estimated number of students .... Course dates ....

B Estimated Income and Expenditure

Costs	Hours	Hourly Rate	Total Basic	ERS Costs	Total Costs
FT lecturer(s) PT lecturer(s) Technicians Admin/clerical Other staff Total staff					
Supplies and services Capital Premises Other costs Total estimated cost					

C Estimated Income ....
Basis of Estimation ....
....

D Invoice Instructions
  (i)   Please invoice the above company for the total fee of ....
  (ii) Invoice individual students according to fees policy............
  (iii) Please invoice on a termly basis in three equal instalments
        YES/NO
  (iv) Other invoice instructions...
        ....

E For the Use of Financial Services Only: Invoicing Details

Invoice No	Date	Amount	Balance O/S	Input MIS Course	Input MIS Fee Details	Other Information

EXERCISE 7: Improving Efficiency and Increasing Income

1   When timetabling there are three resource variables which have to be brought together:
    - programme learning hours;
    - staff learning support hours;
    - room or learning space hours.

    One method that provides a quick indication of the need to investigate the efficiency of any particular area of work further and which will probably lead to efficiency savings is to compare the total of each with the other.

    (a)   Compare the following chart for your college.

Department	Total annual programme learning hours from timetables	Total annual staff learning support hours from timetables	Total annual room hours being used from timetables
Business studies			
Construction			
Total hours	(a)	(b)	(c)

    Columns (a), (b) and (c) above should be equal

    (b)   Compare each of the totals for each department in each of the columns shown above with the totals used to establish budgets, ie staffing and room allocations, as well as programme learning hour inputs agreed through the planning process.

    (c)   Investigate any variance and adjust budgets as necessary.

2   Prepare a spreadsheet showing in rank order, highest first, a list of companies and other organizations contributing to earned income.

3   Suggest ways in which your college may be able to increase its earned income.

    ....
    ....
    ....
    ....
    ....

NOTES:

Inter-College Comparison

8.1 Introduction

To undertake any inter-college comparison, the college must establish a group of ratios or data which are seen as meaningful interpretations of performance. Published information on colleges and college financial reports provide a basis for establishing a view of college performance in relation to other colleges with a similar profile, and a basis for considering what information is required to establish trends and assist strategic decisions. As a general rule, comparative ratios or comparative data give rise to questions rather than provide a definitive answer. It is likely that the differences found will have a number of explanations and in giving rise to questions, may lead to possible answers.

Before reaching conclusions after inter-college comparisons it is important to address the problem of comparability to see how far you are comparing like with like.

For any apparent strength or weakness identified there is generally a range of possible explanations.
Factors which could explain differences could include:

- different student/programme mix;
- college size (economies/diseconomies of scale);
- emphasis of delivery method (traditional teaching v learning support);
- extent of commercial and consultancy activities (full-cost courses);
- quality of provision;
- different geographic location;
- organization variations which cause measurement variations, for example, centralized v decentralized — decentralized could give an apparent reduction in central costs;
- comparisons of financial information shown in the year end accounts can generate questions relating to structure of income,

structure of direct costs and the treatment of indirect costs and non-mainstream operations.

There is also a risk that further education colleges like any other organization facing external analysis, will present an external face which accords with how they wish to be viewed. They may present the information in different forms for different audiences and however, the number of measures possible makes this difficult and does not invalidate their use for comparative purposes.

8.2 Comparing the Size of Your College with Other Colleges

Five useful measures of size are:

- size measured in students attending FEFC programmes;
- size measured by the number of FEFC funding units;
- size measured by the size of the FEFC recurrent funding allocation;
- size measured by *total* income;
- size measured by *total* students.

The following analysis is based on information published by the FEFC. Some estimations have been necessary but every effort has been made to ensure the figures shown are as accurate as possible.

8.2.1 Size Measured in Students Attending FEFC Programmes

Based on 1993/94 targets approximately 2.3 million students attended programmes funded by the Further Education Funding Council (FEFC). Of these approximately 620,000 were students attending whole year full-time courses.

When conversion factors are used to establish full-time equivalent (FTE) numbers the total is shown as almost 900,000 FTE students.

In 1993/94 student targets for each college were expressed as weighted FTE students recognizing for funding purposes a higher weighting for students attending workshop based programmes. Total weighted FTE targets for the sector totalled approximately 1.03 million.

Out of 441 colleges 166 (38 per cent) serve less than 2000 students attending FEFC programmes. Of these 114 colleges (26 per cent) serve less than 1000 students. At the other end of the range thirty-three Colleges serve more than 12,000 FEFC students and of these fourteen colleges more than 15,000 students. Three serve more than 20,000 students.

The following table illustrates the range in the 441 colleges:

	Totals	Smallest college	Medium college	Largest college
Students	2,286,728	107	4,538	35,779
FTE students	887,171	107	1,680	11,412
Weighted FTE students	1,029,678	150	1,942	12,837
Funding units 94/95	131.5m	15,556	246,575	1,377,437

8.2.2 Size Measured in Number of Funding Units in 1994/95 Targets

The FEFC is funding a total of approximately 131.5 million funding units in 1994/95 within 441 colleges. This includes 15,556 units in the smallest college and 1,377,437 units in the largest. Thirty-three per cent (146) colleges have unit targets less than 150,000 units and only twenty-eight colleges (6 per cent) have unit targets over 650,000 units. The medium college ranked 221 has a target of 246,575 units and the college ranked 188 has a target at the 'mean' of 301,250 units.

8.2.3 Size Measured by the Size of the FEFC Total Recurrent Funding Allocation in 1994/95

The FEFC provides approximately 70 per cent of the income required by the colleges in the further education sector. The actual percentage provided in each individual college will depend on the type of college, for example, 70 per cent provided by the FEFC in general further education colleges and 95 per cent in sixth-form colleges.

The largest college in the sector was allocated £28,238,774 in 1994/95 while the smallest was allocated £331,043. The medium college was allocated £4,408,262.

The forty-three (9.8 per cent) largest colleges received an allocation in 1994/95 of more than £10.5million each, of these thirty received more than £12million each and ten more than £16million each. Of the total 441, 115 colleges (26 per cent) received an allocation of less than £3million each and of these fifty-six (13 per cent) received less than £2million each.

In 1993/94 a total of 163 Colleges (37 per cent) received less than £3million each and sixty-five (15 per cent) less than £2million each. The medium received £4,199,288.

8.3 Change in the Average Level of Funding (ALF) between 1993/94 and 1994/95: Efficiency Measured in Cost per Unit of Funding

8.3.1. 1992/93 Units of Funding in £s per Weighted Full Time Equivalent (WFTE) student

Lowest £1486   Medium £2574   Highest £5579

Twelve colleges had a notified unit cost of below £1800 and only thirty-five colleges (8 per cent) had a unit cost below £2000. Ten colleges had a unit cost of above £4000 but only forty-two colleges (9.5 per cent) above £3200. The other 82 per cent of colleges were within the range of £2000 to £3200 with the medium college at £2574.

8.3.2 Average Level of Funding 1993/94 in Funding Units

Twenty-five colleges had an ALF above £30 per funding unit.
Fifty-five colleges (12 per cent) had an ALF above £25 per funding unit.
The medium college had an ALF at £20.03 per unit.
Nineteen colleges had an ALF below £15 per funding unit.
Sixteen colleges were below the £14.50 marginal unit value.

8.3.3 Average Level of Funding 1994/95 in Funding Units

Fifteen colleges had an ALF above £30 per funding unit.
Thirty colleges (7 per cent) had an ALF above £25 per funding unit.
125 colleges (25 per cent) had an ALF over £20.5 per funding unit.
The medium college had an ALF at £18.63 per funding unit.
Thirty-one colleges had an ALF below £15 per funding unit.
Nineteen colleges were below the £14.50 marginal funding unit value.

Annex B provides a table of information to assist the comparison of further education colleges. The colleges are initially ranked with the highest 1994/95 FEFC funding units first and the table shows:

- 1994/95 Funding Units;
- actual WFTE 1992/94 (estimated at the time application for 1994/95 funding units was made to the FEFC but before audit);
- 1993/94 targets (a) weighted FTE (b) FTE (c) actual students;
- 1994/95 recurrent grant;
- 1993/94 recurrent grant;
- average level of funding and unit costs comparison in respect of 1992/93, 1993/94 and 1994/95;
- each college's rank when compared with other colleges is shown for each of the three years, rank 1 being the lowest average level of funding.

EXERCISE 8: Inter College Comparison

The following tables and graphs show numbers of colleges of further education falling in categories in respect of:

(i)   number of units funded by the FEFC for 1994/95;
(ii)   college's recurrent grants for 1994/95;
(iii)   number of FEFC student (targets) in 1993/94;
(iv)   number of FEFC student FTEs (targets) in 1993/94;
(v)   number of FEFC weighted FTE student (targets) in 1993/94;
(vi)   increase/decrease in FEFC recurrent grant (cash) from 1993/94 to 1994/95;
(vii)   percentage change in FEFC recurrent grant from 1993/94 to 1994/95;
(viii) comparison between 1993/94 and 1994/95 average level of funding.

Activity 1 — Using the graphs and the information provided:

(a)   plot the national medium and highest and lowest quartile in each case;
(b)   plot your own College's position on each graph, for comparison and to establish trends;
(c)   note down any further information you consider interesting and which raises questions or which you feel has a strategic value.

Activity 2

Turn to the Table of Information (Annex B) and find your college. List the six colleges immediately above and four colleges below yours on the table.

Obtain information on these colleges, for example, end-of-year report and accounts, together with any other public information available, prospectus, etc. You may wish to obtain information on other colleges of your choice.

Using their end-of-year accounts and reports compare the following with your college:

(a)   Revenue Related Information
   • Operating surplus/deficit to revenue (aggregated, activity related, course related).
   • Other income generating activities (as % of total revenue).

- Structure of aggregate income (for example, of recurrent grant to tuition fees).
- Research grants (as % of total revenue).

(b) Direct Expenditure Related Information
- Direct costs to course-related revenue (recurrent grants, tuition fees, educational contracts and in more detail, academic departments to course-related revenue and academic support departments to course-related revenue).
- Other support services to course related revenue (for example, library, computing, supplies and expenditure per FTE student).

(c) Indirect Expenditure Related
- Indirect expenditure to direct expenditure.
- Administration and general services to course-related revenue and total revenue.
- General education expenditure to course-related revenue.
- Premises to course-related revenue and total revenue.
- Surplus/deficit of residences and catering operations to total revenue and other costs.
- Expenditure in academic departments.
- Expenditure in central services.
- Expenditure in library.

NOTES:

Number of units funded in colleges 1994/95

Units funded 000s 1994/95	Number of colleges
0– 50	13
50– 100	50
100– 150	83
150– 200	40
200– 250	37
250– 300	26
300– 350	30
350– 400	28
400– 450	28
450– 500	20
500– 550	23
550– 600	17
600– 650	10
650– 700	04
700– 750	06
750– 800	05
800– 850	05
850– 900	02
900– 950	03
950–1,000	00
1,000–1,400	03

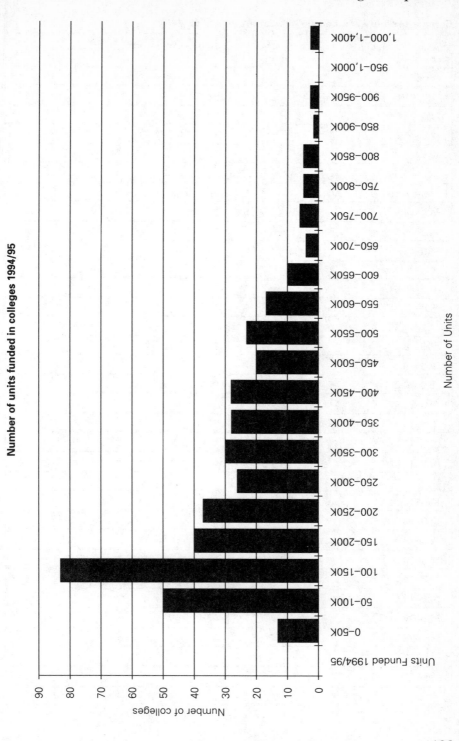

Number of units funded in colleges 1994/95

Units Funded 1994/95

Number of colleges

90 80 70 60 50 40 30 20 10 0

0–50K 50–100K 100–150K 150–200K 200–250K 250–300K 300–350K 350–400K 400–450K 450–500K 500–550K 550–600K 600–650K 650–700K 700–750K 750–800K 800–850K 850–900K 900–950K 950–1,000K 1,000–1,400K

Number of Units

Comparison between college's recurrent grant 1994/95

Recurrent grant £m	Number of colleges
Under 1	04
1.0– 1.5	18
1.5– 2.0	34
2.0– 2.5	49
2.5– 3.0	48
3.0– 3.5	29
3.5– 4.0	18
4.0– 4.5	25
4.5– 5.0	20
5.0– 5.5	26
5.5– 6.0	08
6.0– 6.5	21
6.5– 7.0	19
7.0– 7.5	10
7.5– 8.0	21
8.0– 8.5	11
8.5– 9.0	07
9.0– 9.5	08
9.5–10.0	10
10.0–10.5	12
10.5–11.0	02
11.0–11.5	06
11.5–12.0	05
12.0–12.5	04
12.5–13.0	01
13.0–13.5	06
13.5–14.0	01
14.0–14.5	02
14.5–15.0	02
15.0–15.5	03
15.5–16.0	01
Over 16	10

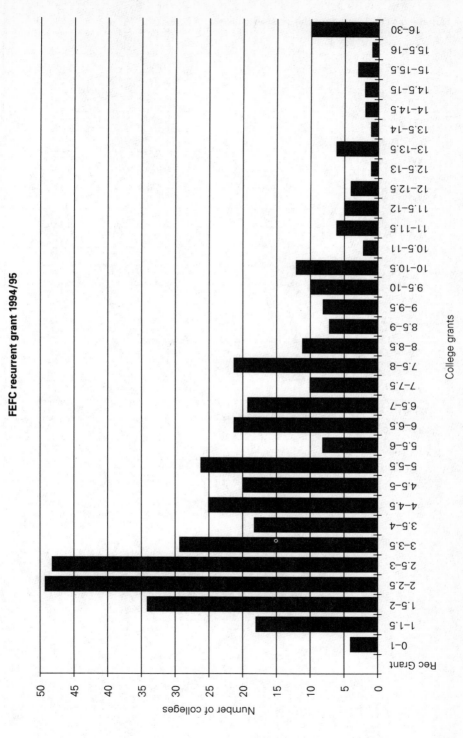

FEFC recurrent grant 1994/95

College grants

Number of colleges

Number of FEFC students (targets) in colleges 1993/94

Number of FEFC students	Number of colleges
0– 1,000	114
1,000– 2,000	52
2,000– 3,000	20
3,000– 4,000	23
4,000– 5,000	37
5,000– 6,000	31
6,000– 7,000	38
7,000– 8,000	28
8,000– 9,000	25
9,000–10,000	14
10,000–11,000	14
11,000–12,000	14
12,000–13,000	6
13,000–14,000	7
14,000–15,000	6
15,000–16,000	2
16,000–17,000	3
17,000–18,000	1
18,000–19,000	3
19,000–20,000	0
Over 20,000	5

Number of FEFC students (targets) in colleges 1993/4

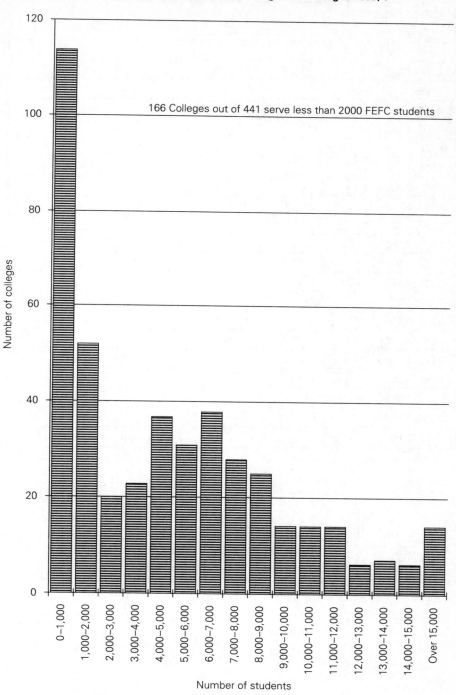

166 Colleges out of 441 serve less than 2000 FEFC students

Number of FTE students (targets) in colleges 1993/94

1993/94 target FTEs	Number of colleges
0– 250	7
250– 500	26
500– 750	49
750–1,000	67
1,000–1,250	26
1,250–1,500	30
1,500–1,750	28
1,750–2,000	22
2,000–2,250	24
2,250–2,500	21
2,500–2,750	24
2,750–3,000	24
3,000–3,250	16
3,250–3,500	18
3,500–3,750	15
3,750–4,000	10
4,000–4,250	11
4,250–4,500	4
4,500–4,750	5
4,750–5,000	5
Over 5,000	13

Target FTEs 1993/94

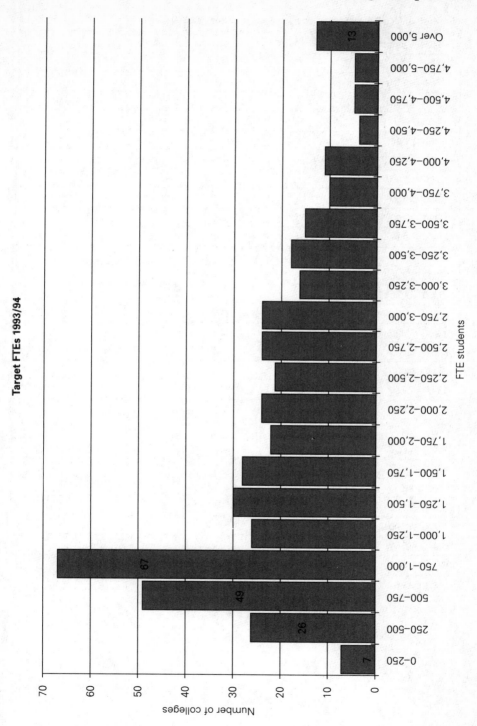

Number of WtFTE students (targets) in colleges 1993/94

1993/94 target WTFTEs	Number of colleges
0– 250	3
250– 500	17
500– 750	38
750–1,000	77
1,000–1,250	28
1,250–1,500	21
1,500–1,750	28
1,750–2,000	22
2,000–2,250	20
2,250–2,500	16
2,500–2,750	15
2,750–3,000	22
3,000–3,250	18
3,250–3,500	20
3,500–3,750	15
3,750–4,000	14
4,000–4,250	17
4,250–4,500	9
4,500–4,750	7
4,750–5,000	9
5,000–5,250	6
5,250–5,500	3
5,500–5,750	4
5,750–6,000	5
6,000–6,250	2
6,250–6,500	1
Over 6,500	8

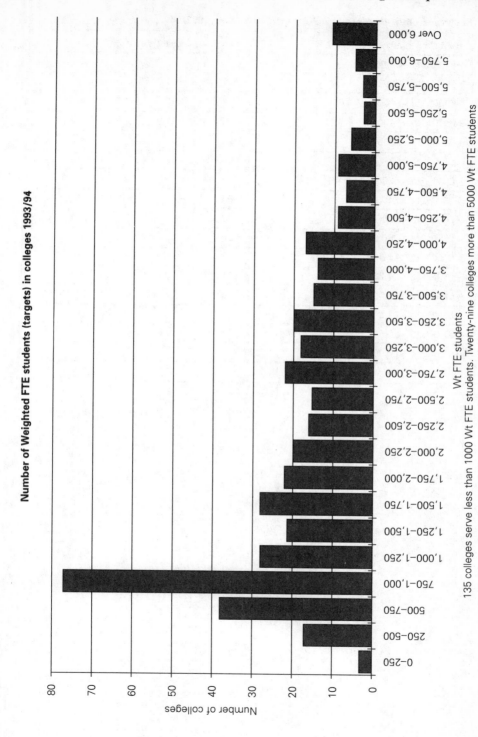

Number of Weighted FTE students (targets) in colleges 1993/94

Number of colleges

Wt FTE students

135 colleges serve less than 1000 Wt FTE students. Twenty-nine colleges more than 5000 Wt FTE students

Recurrent grant increase in colleges 1994/95 over 1993/94

Recurrent grant increase	Number of colleges
−£1,300 to −£1,000	3
−£1,000 to −£800	1
−£800 to −£600	2
−£600 to −£400	6
−£400 to −£200	20
−£200 to £0	60
£0 to +£200	128
+£200 to +£400	94
+£400 to +£600	47
+£600 to +£800	25
+£800 to +£1,000	17
+£1,000 to +£1,200	12
+£1,200 to +£1,400	6
+£1,400 to +£1,600	3
+£1,600 to +£1,800	2
+£1,800 to +£2,000	3
+ Over £2,000	8

Increase/decrease in FEFC recurrent grant from 1993/94 to 1994/95

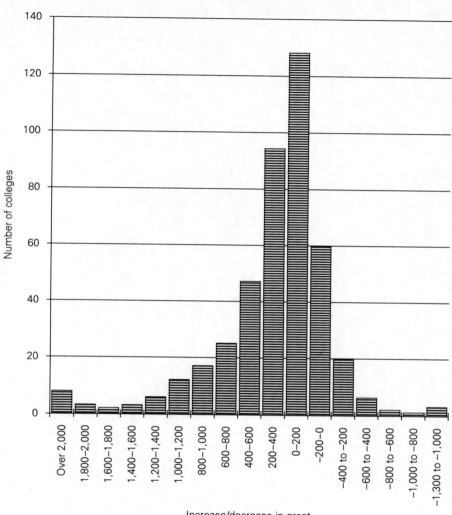

Percentage change in college FEFC funding from 1993/94 to 1994/95

% change			Number of colleges	% of colleges		Total cash increase	Average £m
30%	and	over	9	2.04		24,639,173	£2.738
20	to	30%	17	3.85		23,187,650	£1.364
16	to	20%	17	3.85		10,710,688	£0.630
13	to	16%	24	5.44		17,700,245	£0.738
10	to	13%	31	7.03		16,596,975	
9	to	10%	22	4.99		11,873,140	
8	to	9%	27	6.12		12,183,308	
7	to	8%	24	5.44		9,456,429	
6	to	7%	21	4.76		5,422,238	
5	to	6%	35	7.94		9,246,266	
4	to	5%	27	6.12			
3	to	4%	34	7.71			
2	to	3%	21	4.76			
1	to	2%	22	4.99			
0	to	1%	18	4.08	24.94%		
	0		7	1.59		0	
−2%	to	0%	15	3.40		−739,535	
−4%	to	2%	24	5.44		−3,386,683	
−6%	to	4%	20	4.54		5,751,021	
−9%	to	6%	17	3.85		4,288,633	
Core 10%	to	9%	9	2.04		4,383,588	

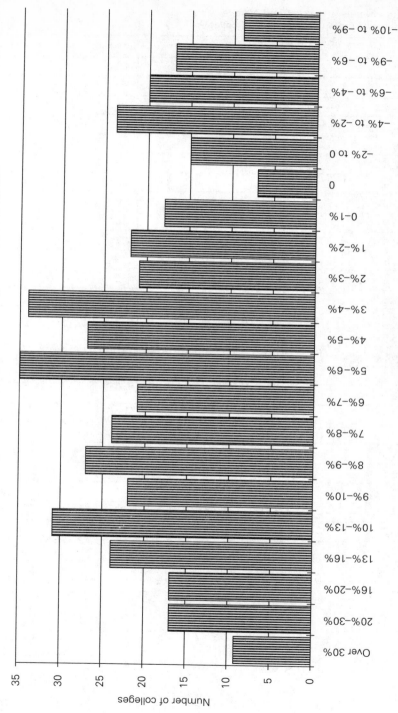

Percentage change in colleges FEFC funding from 1993/94 to 1994/95

Number of colleges

-10% to -9%
-9% to -6%
-6% to -4%
-4% to -2%
-2% to 0
0
0-1%
1%-2%
2%-3%
3%-4%
4%-5%
5%-6%
6%-7%
7%-8%
8%-9%
9%-10%
10%-13%
13%-16%
16%-20%
20%-30%
Over 30%

Percentage change

Eighty-five colleges were given a reduced allocation (18.550m less). A further twenty-five colleges did not receive the full 1% inflation increase. Therefore 109 colleges (approx 25 per cent) out of 441 received less in real terms in 1994/95 than in 1993/94.

**Comparison between 1993/94 and 1994/95
average level of funding — number of colleges**

	1993/94	1994/95
10.5–11.5	01	00
11.5–12.5	02	02
12.5–13.5	02	04
13.5–14.5	11	13
14.5–15.5	13	30
15.5–16.5	29	44
16.5–17.5	29	50
17.5–18.5	35	68
18.5–19.5	67	58
19.5–20.5	56	47
20.5–21.5	45	41
21.5–22.5	31	23
22.5–23.5	35	14
23.5–24.5	19	15
24.5–25.5	14	05
25.5–26.5	08	01
26.5–27.5	08	03
27.5–28.5	06	03
28.5–29.5	04	05
29.5–30.5	02	01
30.5–31.5	04	05
31.5–32.5	03	02
32.5–33.5	01	01
33.5–34.5	04	00
34.5–35.5	04	01
35.5–36.5	02	01
Over 36.5	08	04

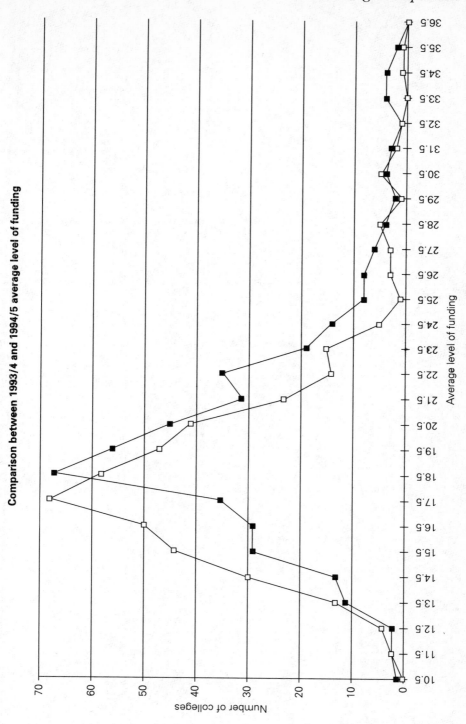

Comparison between 1993/4 and 1994/5 average level of funding

Number of colleges

Average level of funding

Example of End of Year Report and Financial Statements

Report and Financial Statements

for the period from

30 September 1992 to 31 July 1994

Report of the Members of the Corporation for the Period from 30 September 1992 to 31 July 1994

Mission

The College's mission states that:

'We are committed to creating learning opportunities which enable individuals to achieve their personal, educational and employment goals. In doing so, we strive to stimulate the demand for further education among all sectors of the community.

We seek to work with employers to help develop the competence and interests of their employees and to increase the effectiveness of their enterprise.

We aim to serve a national and international community while continuing to be responsive to the needs of our locality.'

Financial Objectives and Review of Out-turn for the Period

In 1992 Parliament passed the **Further and Higher Education Act**. As a result, _____ College of Further Education Corporation came into existence on 30 September 1992. _____College of Further Education was transferred to the Corporation on 1 April 1993. On that date College staff ceased to be employed by _____ County Council and transferred to the employment of the Corporation. Similarly land, buildings and equipment were transferred from the local authority to the ownership of the Corporation.

These financial statements are for the first accounting period of the Corporation ie 30 September 1992 to 31 July 1994, although during the period to 31 March 1993 the Corporation received only transitional funding of £40,000. Transitional funding was used by the Corporation to prepare for independence, in accordance with guidance issued by the Further Education Funding Council (FEFC).

The members of the Corporation planned for and achieved an operational surplus for the period, while making provision for a planned maintenance programme, remodelling of existing buildings and the purchase of computer equipment.

Developments

Members planned to increase student numbers by 8 per cent during the 1993–94 academic year over the 1992–93 level. This growth was achieved and 15,091 students studied at the college during that year of whom just over 2000 were full-time.

During the 1992–93 academic year, the agreed outcomes of an organizational review were successfully implemented. These changes were designed to ensure that the College could respond to the significant curriculum changes which were taking place in further education, as well as to fulfil the requirements of incorporation.

In September 1992 the FEFC conducted a sector-wide survey of the condition of College buildings. Hunter and Partners were contracted to undertake the survey.

The survey determined the condition of the College's buildings and placed the cost of the necessary remedial work in three main categories, the first of which was subdivided into two.

- *Priority 1(a)*: Items of urgent work relating to breaches of legislation which should be undertaken as soon as possible and certainly within one year of the date of survey. This includes work relating to health and safety of occupants, fire regulation and environmental health requirements, particularly where premises have been given recommendations for the remedy of deficiencies.
- *Priority 1(b)*: Items of urgent repair work which should be carried out within one year of the date of survey.
- *Priority 2*: Items of work to be undertaken within two years of the date of survey to maintain the use and value of the building.
- *Priority 3*: All items of work identified to be undertaken within five years of the date of the survey in order to maintain the condition of the buildings.

The Hunter programme (priorities 1(a), and 1(b) and 2) are being partly funded by the FEFC. During the period covered by this Report, the College has completed all Priority 1(a) work, and most of 1(b), and is progressing well with Priority 2 work.

Following a full inspection by Her Majesty's Inspectors, the College installed a fibreoptic network during the 1992–93 academic year and purchased additional computing equipment in order to increase the availability of information technology to students and staff.

Future Developments

The College will soon enter into partnership with _____ City Council on the establishment of the _____ Training Centre. The College will manage the facility under contract to the Council. The centre itself remains the property of the City Council.

The College is actively seeking funding from outside bodies (perhaps in partnership with the City Council and other organizations) for the creation of (i) performing arts and (ii) sports facilities. At the moment, the further development of the College curriculum is hampered by this lack of facilities.

The College is also seeking partnership with local firms in the establishment of a crèche. Discussions, at the time of writing, are still taking place.

Post Balance Sheet Events

There have been no significant post balance sheet events.

Employment of Disabled Persons

The Corporation adopted its Equal Opportunities policy during the period covered by this Report. The College considers all applications from disabled persons, bearing in mind the aptitudes of the individuals concerned. Where an existing employee becomes disabled every effort is made to ensure that employment with the College continues. The College's policy is to provide training, career development and opportunities for promotion which are, as far as possible, identical to those for other employees.

Staff and Student Involvement

The College has a thriving Students' Association with elected officers and a delegated budget. Students are represented on the Academic Board of the College and there is a student member of the governing body. The College encourages staff involvement in the decision making processes of the College, all groups of staff being represented on the Academic Board. There are two elected staff members of the governing body.

Charitable and Taxation Status

The College is an exempt charity for the purposes of the Charities Act 1960 and is not liable to corporation tax.

Professional Advisers

External auditors
Internal auditors
Bankers
Solicitors

Members

The members who served the Corporation during the period were as follows:

Income and Expenditure Account

For the period from 30 September 1992 to 31 July 1994

	Notes	*1994* *£'000*
Income		
FEFC grants	1	11,907
Education contracts	2	1,475
Tuition fees and charges	3	2,542
Other grant income	4	162
Other operating income	5	1,214
Investment income	6	120
Total Income		17,420
Expenditure		
Staff costs	7	12,896
Other operating expenses	9	3,674
Depreciation	12	562
Interest payable	10	2
Total expenditure		17,134
Surplus on continuing operations after depreciation of assets at valuation and before tax		286
Taxation	11	—
Surplus on continuing operations after depreciation of assets at valuation and tax	20	286

Statement of Total Recognised Gains and Losses

For the period from 30 September 1992 to 31 July 1994

	Notes	1994 £'000
Surplus on continuing operations after depreciation of assets at valuation and tax		286
Unrealized surplus on revaluation of fixed assets	12	11,814
Accumulated balance transferred on vesting day from the local education authority	20	1,027
Total recognised gains relating to the period		13,127

Statement of Historical Cost Surpluses and Deficits

For the period from 30 September 1992 to 31 July 1994

	Notes	1994 £'000
Surplus on continuing operations after depreciation of assets at valuation and tax		286
Difference between historical cost depreciation and the actual charge for the period calculated on the revalued amount	19	456
Historical cost surplus for the period		742

Balance Sheet

As at 31 July 1994

	Notes	1994 £'000	1994 £'000
Fixed assets			
Tangible assets	12		12,063
Current assets			
Stock		18	
Debtors	13	619	
Short term investments	14	2,250	
Cash at bank and in hand		3	
		2,890	
Creditors: amounts falling due within one year	15	1,365	
Net current assets			1,525
Total assets less current liabilities			13,588
Provisions for liabilities and charges	16		208
Deferred capital grants	17		248
Net assets			13,132
Reserves			
Restricted reserves	18		5
Revaluation reserves	19		11,358
Income and expenditure account	20		1,769
			13,132

The Financial Statements on pages 6 to 21 were approved by the Corporation on 9 November 1994 and were signed on its behalf on that day by:

Chairman   Principal

Example of End of Year Report and Financial Statements

Cash Flow Statement

For the period from 30 September 1992 to 31 July 1994

	Notes	1994 £'000
Net cash inflow from operating activities	22	1,244
Returns on investments and servicing of finance		
Income from short term investments	6	111
Other interest received	6	9
Interest paid	10	(2)
Net cash inflow from returns on investments and servicing of finance		118
Tax paid	11	—
Investing activities		
Payments to acquire tangible fixed assets	12	(812)
Deferred capital grants received	17	300
Proceeds of sale of tangible fixed assets		11
Net cash outflow from investing activities		(501)
Net cash inflow before financing		861
Financing		
Restricted reserves (trust and other funds)	18	5
Accumulated balance transferred on vesting day from the local education authority	20	1,027
Net cash inflow from financing activities		1,032
Increase in cash and cash equivalents	23	1,893

Statement of Accounting Policies

Basis of Preparation

These financial statements have been prepared in accordance with FEFC Circular (94/13) and in accordance with applicable accounting standards.

Basis of Accounting

The financial statements are prepared in accordance with the historical cost convention modified by the revaluation of certain fixed assets.

Recognition of Income

Income from research grants, contracts and other services rendered is included to the extent of the completion of the contract or service concerned. All income from short-term deposits is credited to the income and expenditure account in the period in which it is earned.

Pension Schemes

Retirement benefits to employees of the College are provided by the Teachers Superannuation Scheme (TSS) and the _____ County Council Superannuation Fund which is a Local Government Superannuation Scheme (LGSS). These are defined benefit schemes which are contracted out of the State Earnings Related Pension Scheme. Contributions to the schemes are charged to the income and expenditure account so as to spread the cost of pensions over employees' working lives with the College in such a way that the pension cost is a substantially level percentage of current and future pensionable payroll. The contributions to the LGSS are determined by a qualified actuary on the basis of triennial valuations using the projected unit method. The contributions to the TSS are determined by the Government Actuary.

Tangible Fixed Assets

(a)   Land and Buildings

Land and buildings inherited from the local education authority are stated in the balance sheet at valuation on the basis of the existing use open market value. Land and buildings acquired since incorporation are included in the balance sheet at cost. Freehold land is not depreciated. Freehold buildings are depreciated on a straight line basis over their expected useful economic life to the college of fifty years. Leasehold land and buildings are amortized over fifty years or, if shorter, the period of the lease.

(b) Equipment

Equipment costing less than £500 per individual item is written off to the income and expenditure account in the period of acquisition. All other equipment is capitalized at cost. Equipment inherited from the local education authority is included in the balance sheet at valuation.

Equipment is depreciated on a straight line basis over its useful economic life as follows:

Motor vehicles	4 years
General equipment	10 years
Computer equipment	3 years

Where equipment is acquired with the aid of specific grants it is capitalised and depreciated in accordance with the above policy, with the related grant being credited to a deferred capital grant account and released to the income and expenditure account over the expected useful economic life of the related equipment.

Leased Assets

Costs in respect of operating leases are charged on a straight line basis over the lease term. Leasing agreements which transfer to the College substantially all the benefits and risks of ownership of an asset (ie finance leases) are treated as if the asset had been purchased outright. The assets are included in fixed assets and the capital element of the leasing commitments are shown as obligations under finance leases. The lease rentals are treated as consisting of capital and interest elements. The capital element is applied to reduce the outstanding obligations and the interest element is charged to the income and expenditure account in proportion to the reducing capital element outstanding. Assets held under finance leases are depreciated over the shorter of the lease term or the useful economic lives of equivalent owned assets. Assets which are held under hire purchase contracts which have the characteristics of finance leases are depreciated over their useful lives.

Statement of Accounting Policies

Investments

Current asset investments are included in the balance sheet at the lower of their original cost and net realisable value.

Stocks

Stocks are stated at the lower of their cost and net realizable value. Where necessary, provision is made for obsolete, slow moving and defective stocks.

Maintenance of Premises

The cost of routine corrective maintenance is charged to the income and expenditure account in the period it is incurred. The college has a five-year planned maintenance programme which is reviewed on an annual basis. The expected costs of carrying out planned maintenance are charged as a provision to the income and expenditure account on a systematic and rational basis over this period with a view to spreading the cost of the maintenance evenly over the life of the maintenance plan. Actual expenditure on planned maintenance is charged to the provision.

Foreign Currency Translation

Assets and liabilities denominated in foreign currencies are translated at the rates of exchange ruling at the end of the financial period with all resulting exchange differences being taken to the income and expenditure account in the period in which they arise.

Taxation

As an exempt charity the college benefits by being broadly exempt from corporation tax on income it receives from tuition fees, interest and rents.

The college is exempted from levying VAT on most of the services it provides to students. For this reason the college is generally unable to recover input VAT it suffers on goods and services purchased.

Notes to the Financial Statements

For the period from 30 September 1992 to 31 July 1994

1 Further Education Funding Council Grants

	1994 £'000
Recurrent grant	11,533
Income for payments made under Section 6 (5) of the Further and Higher Education Act 1992	265
Releases of deferred capital grants (FEFC)	52
Transitional income for the period 30 September 1992 to 31 March 1993	40
Access funds	14
Restructuring fund	3
	11,907

During the 1993–94 academic year the college received £13,884 from the FEFC as access funds. These funds were used for the defined purposes of student support, and were administered in accordance with the terms and conditions specified by the FEFC.

2 Education Contracts

	1994 £'000
TEC — Work-related further education	483
TEC — Other	40
Managing agencies	346
Higher education institutions	65
Local education authority	44
Other educational income	497
	1,475

3 Tuition Fees and Charges

	1994 £'000
Home and EU	2,422
Non-EU	120
	2,542

Home and EU include summer term tuition fees for the 1992/93 academic year of £345,704 which were invoiced before 31 March 1993.

4 Other Grant Income

	1994 £'000
European funds	17
Other funds	145
	162

5 Other Operating Income

	1994 £'000
Catering and residence operations	430
Other income generating activities	248
Profit on disposal of tangible fixed assets	10
Other income	526
	1,214

6 Investment Income

	1994 £'000
Income from short-term investments	111
Other interest receivable	9
	120

7 Staff Costs

The table below analyzes the average number of persons (including senior post holders) employed by the college during the period, expressed as full-time equivalents:

	1994 *Number* *of full-time* *equivalents*
Teaching departments	392
Teaching support services	24
Other support services	34
Administration and central services	36
Premises	63
Other	17
	566

Staff costs for the above persons:

The table below analyses the employment costs for the period of these employees, including senior post holders.

	1994 *£'000*
Teaching departments	9,501
Teaching support services	389
Other support services	481
Administration and central services	1,167
Premises	678
Catering and residences	212
Other income-generating activities	192
Miscellaneous	87
Staff restructuring	189
	12,896

	1994 *£'000*
Wages and salaries	11,355
Social security costs	881
Other pension costs	660
	12,896

	1994
	£'000

Employment costs for staff on permanent contracts	10,882
Employment costs for staff on short-term and temporary contracts	1,825
Restructuring costs	189
	12,896

8   Emoluments of Senior Postholders and Members

The information below relating to the senior postholders is for the sixteen months 1 April 1993 to 31 July 1994:

	1994
	£

Emoluments including pension contributions	_____
Emoluments including pension contributions, paid to the Principal	_____

The Principal's emoluments comprise basic salary at the rate of _____ per annum for the sixteen months, arrears from a Performance Related Pay scheme which ended on 31 March 1993, and employers normal contributions to the Teachers Superannuation Scheme at 8.05 per cent. Other senior postholders' emoluments are presented on the same basis.

There were no benefits in kind paid to the senior postholders.

Other than the Principal and the elected staff members of the Corporation, no other members of the Corporation received any payment from the college during the period 30 September 1992 to 31 July 1994 other than for the reimbursement of travel and subsistence expenses incurred in the course of their duties.

The number of senior postholders who received emoluments including pension contributions for the sixteen months 1 April 1993 to 31 July 1994, in the following ranges was:

	1994 *Number*
	1
	2
	1

9   Other Operating Expenses

	1994 *£'000*
Teaching departments	927
Teaching support services	147
Other support services	57
General education expenditure	238
Administration and central services	690
Premises costs	755
Planned maintenance	200
Payments made under Section 6 (5) of the Further and Higher Education Act 1992	265
Transitional expenditure for the period 30 September 1992 to 31 March 1993	40
Other expenses	355
	3,674

Other operating expenses include:

	1994 *£'000*
Auditors' remuneration:	
— external audit	8
— internal audit	11
— other services both external and internal	12
Hire of plant and machinery — operating leases	61
Hire of other assets — operating leases	53

10 Interest Payable

	1994 £'000
On bank loans, overdrafts and other loans:	
Repayable within 5 years, not by instalments	2

11 Taxation

The members of the Corporation do not believe the College was liable for any corporation tax arising out of its activities during this period.

12 Tangible Fixed Assets

	Freehold land and buildings £'000	Equipment £'000	Motor vehicles £'000	Total £'000
Cost or valuation				
At 30 September 1992	—	—	—	—
Additions at cost	—	812	—	812
Inherited additions at valuation	11,038	769	7	11,814
Disposals	—	(1)	—	(1)
At 31 July 1994	11,038	1,580	7	12,625
Depreciation				
At 30 September 1992	—	—	—	—
Charge for period	(163)	(396)	(3)	(562)
Eliminated in respect of disposals	—	—	—	—
At 31 July 1994	(163)	(396)	(3)	(562)
Net book value				
At 31 July 1994	10,875	1,184	4	12,063
Net book value				
At 30 September 1992	—	—	—	—

Analysis of Net Book Value as at 31 July 1994

Inherited	10,875	479	4	11,358
Financed by capital grant	—	238	—	238
Other	—	467	—	467
	10,875	1,184	4	12,063

At the balance sheet date, the title deed relating to land and buildings inherited from the local authority on vesting day had not been received. The registration process is expected to be completed shortly and the assets have been included in these accounts.

Land and buildings were valued for the purpose of the 1994 financial statements at existing use open market value by a firm of independent chartered surveyors. Other tangible fixed assets inherited from the local education authority on vesting day have been valued by the Corporation on a depreciated original cost basis.

Land and buildings with a net book value of £10,875,000 have been funded from local education authority sources. Should these assets be sold, the College would either have to surrender the sale proceeds to the FEFC or use them in accordance with the financial memorandum agreed with the FEFC.

13 Debtors

1994
£'000

Amounts Falling Due Within One Year

Trade debtors	329
Prepayments and accrued income	290
	619

14 Short Term Investments

Short term investments of £2,250,000 are represented by funds on the money market with maturity dates ranging from 1 day to 31 days.

15 Creditors: Amounts Falling Due within One Year

	1994 £'000
Bank overdraft	360
Payments received on account	230
Trade creditors	324
Other taxation and social security	293
Accruals	158
	1,365

16 Provisions for Liabilities and Charges

	Planned maintenance £'000	Other provisions £'000	Total £'000
At 30 September 1992	—	—	—
Transferred from income and expenditure account	200	153	353
Expenditure in the period	(145)	—	(145)
At 31 July 1994	55	153	208

The provision for planned maintenance is derived from the planned maintenance programme (PMP) prepared by the college's estates manager, following a full survey of each building in the college's estate.

Other provisions are for enhanced future pensions for former employees, and the excess of the accumulated pension cost over payment of contributions to the local government superannuation scheme for existing employees (note 21).

17 Deferred Capital Grants

	1994 £'000
At 30 September 1992	—
Cash received from FEFC	300
Released to income and expenditure account	(52)
At 31 July 1994	248

18 Restricted Reserves

The following trust and other funds are an integral part of the College:

	Capital	Revenue	1994 Total
	£	£	£
Trusts			
Jane Belcher Award	1,000	114	1,114
Other Funds			
Caring Award	1,000	37	1,037
Desmond Keohane Bequest	500	119	619
Lower Bequest	500	28	528
Student Welfare Fund	1,000	712	1,712
	4,000	1,010	5,010

Trust and other funds are represented by cash balances and short term investments held by the College.

The Threshold Trust is also associated with the College, but not consolidated with these accounts. The principal capital for this trust derived from the J.F. Turnbull Bequest. At the year end, this trust had a balance of £10,098, represented by cash and investments held independently of the College.

19 Revaluation Reserve

	1994 £'000
At 30 September 1992	—
Inherited assets acquired at valuation	11,814
Transfer from revaluation reserve to income and expenditure account	(456)
At 31 July 1994	11,358

20 Income and Expenditure Account

	1994 £'000	1994 £'000
At 30 September 1992		—
Accumulated balance transferred on vesting day from the local education authority:		
— debtors	746	
— cash	299	
— stock	6	
— less creditors	(24)	
		1,027
Transfer to income and expenditure account from revaluation reserve		456
Surplus on continuing operations after depreciation of assets at valuation and tax		286
At 31 July 1994		1,769

21 Pension and Similar Obligations

The College's employees belong to two principal pension schemes, the Teachers Superannuation Scheme (TSS) and the Local Government Superannuation Scheme (LGSS), which are both of the defined benefit type. The total pension cost was £659,787.

Teachers Superannuation Scheme

Although teachers are employed by the College, their retirement and other superannuation benefits, including annual increases payable under the Pensions (Increase) Acts, are, as provided for in the Superannuation Act 1972, paid out of monies provided by Parliament. Under the TSS, which is an unfunded scheme, teachers' contributions, on a 'pay-as-you-go' basis, and employers' contributions are credited to the Exchequer under arrangements governed by the above Act.

The latest actuarial review of the TSS, carried out by the Government Actuary using normal actuarial principals, was as at 31 March 1986. The aim of the review was to specify the level of future contributions. The cost of pension increases was excluded from the valuation and, consequently, neither teachers nor their employers contribute to this added value which is met directly by the Exchequer.

The value of the assets (estimated future contributions together with the proceeds from the notional investments held at the valuation date) was £30,138 million. Compared with the total liabilities (pensions currently at payment and the estimated cost of future payments), there was a deficiency of £1552 million, which required a supplementary employers' contribution of 0.75 per cent commencing on 1 April 1989. The contributions throughout the period were 6 per cent for the employees and 8.05 per cent for the employers.

Local Government Superannuation Scheme

The assets of the scheme are held in a separate trustee-administered fund. The pension costs are assessed in accordance with the advice of independent qualified actuaries using the projected unit method. The latest actuarial valuation of the LGSS was as at 31 March 1992. The assumptions that have the most significant effect on the valuation and other relevant data for the scheme as a whole are as follows:

Rate of return on investments	9.0%
Rate of increase in salaries	6.5%
Rate of increase in pensions	4.5%
Rate of increase in dividends	4.5%
Market value of the assets at the date of the last valuation	£250m

The actuarial value of the assets represented 105 per cent of the benefits which had accrued to members after allowing for future increases in earnings.

An amount of £53,348 is included in provisions, which represents the excess of the accumulated pension cost over the payment of contributions to the funds (note 16).

22 Reconciliation of Operating Surplus to Net Cash Inflow from Operating Activities

	Notes	£'000
Surplus on continuing operations after depreciation of assets at valuation and tax		286
Deferred capital grants released to income	1	(52)
Profit on disposal of tangible fixed assets	5	(10)
Income from short term investments	6	(111)
Interest receivable	6	(9)
Interest payable	10	2
Depreciation	12	562

(Increase) in stock		(18)
(Increase) in debtors	13	(329)
(Increase) in pre-payments and accrued income	13	(290)
Increase in payments received on account	15	230
Increase in trade creditors	15	324
Increase in other taxation and social security	15	293
Increase in accruals	15	158
Increase in provisions	16	208
Net cash inflow from operating activities		1,244

23 Cash and Cash Equivalents

	1994
	£'000

Changes during the period

At 30 September 1992	—
Net cash inflow	1,893
At 31 July 1994	1,893

Analysis of balances

Cash at bank and in hand	3
Bank overdraft	(360)
Short-term investments	2,250
At 31 July 1994	1,893

24 Post Balance Sheet Events

Details of post balance sheet events are given in the report of the members of the Corporation.

25 Capital Commitments

	1994
	£'000

Commitments contracted for at 31 July 1994	23
Authorized but not contracted for at 31 July 1994	223

26 Financial Comments

At 31 July 1994 the College had annual commitments under non-cancellable operating leases as follows:

	Land and Buildings £'000	Other £'000
Expiring within one year	14	19
Expiring between two and five years inclusive	27	39
	41	58

Description of the Responsibilities of the Members of the Corporation

The members of the Corporation of the College are required to present audited financial statements for each financial year.

Within the terms and conditions of the Financial Memorandum agreed between the Further Education Funding Council (the Council) and the Corporation of the College, the Corporation, through its chief officer, is required to prepare financial statements for each financial year, which give a true and fair view of the state of affairs of the College and the surplus for that year.

In preparing the financial statements the Corporation is required to:

- select suitable accounting policies and then apply them consistently;
- make judgments and estimates that are reasonable and prudent;
- state whether applicable accounting standards have been followed, subject to any material departures disclosed and explained in the financial statements;
- prepare financial statements on the going concern basis unless it is inappropriate to assume that the College will continue in operation.

The Corporation is responsible for keeping proper accounting records which disclose with reasonable accuracy at any time the financial position of the College and to enable it to ensure that the financial statements are prepared in accordance with the relevant legislation of incorporation and other relevant accounting standards. It has general responsibility for taking such steps that are reasonably open to it to safeguard assets of the College and to prevent and detect fraud and other irregularities.

Members of the Corporation are responsible for ensuring that funds from the Council are used only in accordance with the Financial Memorandum with the Council and any other conditions which the Council may from time to time prescribe. Members of the Corporation must ensure that there are appropriate financial and management controls in place sufficient to safeguard public funds and ensure that they are used only in accordance with the conditions under which they have been made available. In addition, members of the Corporation are responsible for securing the economical, efficient and effective management of the College's resources and expenditure, so that the benefits that should be derived from the application of public funds by the Council are not put at risk.

Auditors' Report to the members of the Corporation

We have audited the financial statements on pages 154 to 173 which have been prepared in accordance with the accounting policies set out on pages 158 and 160.

Respective Responsibilities of the Members of the Corporation and Auditors

As described on page 174, the members of the Corporation are responsible for the preparation of the financial statements. It is our responsibility to form an independent opinion, based on our audit, on those statements and to report our opinion to you.

Basis of Our Opinion

We conducted our audit in accordance with auditing standards issued by the Auditing Practices Board. An audit includes examination, on a test basis, of evidence relevant to the amounts and disclosures in the financial statements. It also includes an assessment of the significant estimates and judgments made by the members of the Corporation in the preparation of the financial statements, and of whether the accounting policies are appropriate to the College's circumstances, consistently applied and adequately disclosed.

We planned and performed our audit so as to obtain all the information and explanations which we considered necessary in order to provide us with sufficient evidence to give reasonable assurance that the financial statements are free from material misstatement, whether caused by fraud or other irregularity or error. In forming our opinion we also evaluated the overall adequacy of the presentation of information in the financial statements.

Opinion

In our opinion the financial statements give a true and fair view of the state of the college's affairs as at 31 July 1994 and of its surplus of income over expenditure for the period then ended.

In our opinion funds from whatever source administered by the college for specific purposes have been properly applied for the intended purposes and, where relevant, managed in accordance with appropriate legislation for the period ended 31 July 1994.

In our opinion funds provided by the FEFC have been applied in accordance with the financial memorandum and any other terms and conditions attached to them for the period ended 31 July 1994.

Spreadsheet Comparisons of all Colleges

Comparison of Further Education Colleges Ordered Highest 94/95 Funding Units First

06-Sep-94

Count	College	94/95 Funding Units	93/4 Actual Wt FTE	93/94 Wt FTE Target	93/94 Target FTE	93/94 Target Students	94/95 Recurrent Grant	93/94 Recurrent Grant	ALF 94/95	ALF 93/94	Unit Cost 92/93	94/95 ALF Rank	93/94 ALF Rank	92/93 Unit Cost Rank
1	Sheffield College (The)	1,377,437	12,124	12,837	11,412	35,779	£28,238,774	£29,538,467	£20.50	£23.56	£2,769	317	358	299
2	City of Liverpool Community College	1,201,963	10,154	9,960	8,561	25,925	£24,018,311	£22,809,412	£19.98	£21.52	£2,926	297	291	341
3	Stoke-On-Trent College	1,115,827	7,772	7,131	5,775	16,239	£18,644,790	£14,265,333	£16.70	£17.72	£2,259	100	98	96
4	Newcastle College	935,695	7,114	6,928	5,595	13,132	£16,958,844	£13,470,091	£18.12	£19.71	£2,491	186	202	174
5	City & Islington College	918,798	7,806	7,541	6,697	20,760	£20,264,212	£18,938,516	£22.05	£22.57	£0	370	325	425
6	Barnsley College	903,970	7,176	5,814	4,997	13,518	£13,401,276	£9,774,818	£14.82	£12.18	£1,974	24	3	30
7	Wigan & Leigh College	867,267	6,269	7,203	6,204	15,349	£17,524,199	£18,388,456	£20.20	£24.81	£2,847	302	379	325
8	Preston College	864,199	5,882	5,718	4,875	14,344	£11,835,929	£10,409,788	£13.69	£13.58	£2,127	9	6	58
9	Mid-Kent College of Higher & Further Education	831,910	5,009	4,558	3,908	7,886	£13,367,571	£9,750,234	£16.06	£16.52	£2,563	76	59	207
10	Bradford & Ilkley Community College	814,842	6,114	5,864	4,979	21,206	£17,584,917	£15,913,952	£21.58	£22.93	£3,295	361	342	388
11	City College, Manchester	807,164	6,395	5,818	4,873	11,905	£12,124,794	£9,857,556	£15.02	£15.60		34	31	447
12	Wirral Metropolitan College	806,589	7,626	7,647	6,681	26,488	£15,247,710	£15,096,743	£18.90	£22.48	£2,687	245	321	266
13	Handsworth College	805,588	5,629	3,674	3,036	10,176	£10,245,997	£5,698,552	£12.71	£7.44	£1,621	3	1	3
14	Hull College	789,927	6,611	6,193	5,239	16,298	£13,409,199	£12,335,970	£16.97	£17.38	£2,333	113	86	122
15	Blackburn College	780,060	6,164	6,063	5,063	14,188	£12,380,111	£11,548,611	£15.87	£16.53	£2,283	62	60	106
16	Croydon College	772,412	5,052	5,147	4,341	10,614	£15,723,095	£14,903,408	£20.35	£21.97	£2,984	312	310	353
17	Manchester College of Arts & Technology	753,413	6,717	6,559	5,617	18,278	£13,426,776	£12,763,095	£17.82	£19.57	£2,640	159	193	248
18	Bournemouth & Poole College of Further Education	750,562	5,445	5,671	4,928	10,626	£13,347,755	£13,228,697	£17.78	£19.24	£2,509	157	176	181
19	Swindon College	748,256	5,223	5,312	4,476	14,727	£9,992,774	£9,427,145	£13.35	£13.81	£1,886	5	8	24
20	West Herts. College	744,101	5,485	5,332	4,569	11,926	£14,438,366	£13,307,250	£19.40	£20.24	£2,747	258	235	292
21	Sandwell College of Further & Higher Education	736,986	5,262	5,056	4,222	12,811	£17,041,878	£16,773,502	£23.12	£25.68	£4,664	392	391	419
22	Oaklands College	718,084	5,974	5,957	5,074	13,996	£14,163,184	£13,724,016	£19.72	£21.09	£2,639	285	271	247
23	College of North West London (The)	709,395	6,394	5,679	4,672	14,156	£17,119,065	£16,636,603	£24.13	£22.72	£2,936	403	331	345
24	South Thames College	707,447	5,487	5,018	4,444	16,439	£15,204,884	£13,221,638	£21.49	£20.63	£2,227	357	250	88
25	Blackpool & the Fylde College	690,945	5,333	4,865	4,132	12,331	£11,949,009	£10,952,346	£17.29	£18.82	£2,475	127	142	165
26	East Berkshire College	690,838	5,175	5,243	4,513	14,157	£11,613,647	£10,763,343	£16.81	£17.65	£2,425	105	95	151
27	Clarendon College	689,078	4,132	3,688	3,302	12,618	£9,409,710	£6,349,332	£13.65	£13.05	£1,793	8	4	12
28	Wakefield College	679,255	6,138	6,424	5,593	18,945	£14,604,890	£14,517,783	£21.50	£24.43	£2,761	358	373	296

Comparison of Further Education Colleges Ordered Highest 94/95 Funding Units First

06-Sep-94

Count	College	94/95 Funding Units	93/4 Actual Wt FTE	93/94 Wt FTE Target	93/94 Target FTE	93/94 Target Students	94/95 Recurrent Grant	93/94 Recurrent Grant	ALF 94/95	ALF 93/94	Unit Cost 92/93	94/95 ALF Rank	93/94 ALF Rank	92/93 Unit Cost Rank
29	St Helens College	635,629	4,852	4,687	3,857	11,963	£13,098,329	£12,128,082	£20.60	£23.26	£2,987	322	349	355
30	Lambeth College	623,000	4,907	4,976	4,197	11,109	£17,517,080	£17,378,056	£28.11	£30.92	£3,356	420	419	391
31	Lewisham College	621,959	4,008	4,191	3,478	8,956	£15,127,321	£14,672,474	£24.32	£25.64	£3,309	406	390	390
32	Huddersfield Technical College	618,640	5,222	5,090	4,271	13,502	£11,693,565	£11,298,130	£18.90	£19.90	£2,662	246	212	255
33	South Devon College	613,658	4,086	4,466	3,908	6,811	£8,447,438	£7,778,488	£13.76	£15.55	£1,966	11	30	28
34	Park Lane College	613,063	3,398	3,863	3,670	11,915	£9,739,074	£7,917,946	£15.88	£17.73	£1,518	63	99	2
35	West Kent College	610,964	4,635	4,727	4,076	6,081	£9,093,085	£8,319,382	£14.88	£16.02	£2,082	28	42	49
36	Solihull College, The	610,125	5,158	5,382	4,705	14,995	£10,159,695	£9,873,367	£16.65	£17.95	£2,052	97	105	44
37	Gloucester College of Arts & Technology	603,858	4,893	4,906	4,201	11,010	£11,229,686	£10,340,411	£18.59	£20.04	£2,463	218	222	163
38	Havering College of Further & Higher Education	601,351	3,849	4,040	3,438	7,682	£9,807,926	£9,701,213	£16.31	£16.81	£2,409	80	68	145
39	Ealing Tertiary College	599,096	4,742	5,513	4,622	11,415	£12,065,104	£13,272,942	£20.13	£23.55	£0	301	357	431
40	Cambridge Regional College	595,390	4,925	4,884	4,241	9,214	£11,676,125	£11,380,239	£19.61	£21.68	£2,300	277	298	113
41	South East Essex College of Arts & Technology	594,392	4,386	4,192	3,437	6,079	£10,153,724	£8,377,660	£17.08	£18.55	£2,444	119	127	155
42	Bilston Community College	593,648	5,844	4,977	4,246	18,013	£9,788,196	£8,906,457	£16.48	£16.94	£2,056	92	75	45
43	Dudley College of Technology	592,475	5,714	5,928	5,023	17,477	£9,719,977	£9,623,740	£16.40	£18.24	£1,807	88	115	13
44	Highbury College of Technology	591,389	4,296	4,649	3,733	10,396	£11,097,007	£11,780,262	£18.76	£21.29	£2,972	234	280	352
45	Suffolk College	581,411	4,893	4,962	4,183	11,598	£10,467,517	£10,202,258	£18.00	£19.24	£2,494	174	178	176
46	Matthew Boulton College of Further & Higher Ed.	580,351	3,754	3,775	3,132	8,204	£8,237,718	£7,374,859	£14.19	£14.79	£2,622	15	18	233
47	South Tyneside College	576,694	4,990	5,032	4,238	13,386	£11,030,579	£10,667,871	£19.12	£20.39	£2,484	256	242	170
48	Norwich City College of Further & Higher Education	574,092	4,641	4,616	3,945	8,496	£12,218,593	£11,658,963	£21.28	£23.33	£3,119	347	351	373
49	Oxford College of Further Education	569,454	4,172	4,183	3,491	10,188	£9,289,835	£8,813,885	£16.31	£17.97	£2,378	79	106	132
50	College of North East London (The)	561,987	3,691	3,537	2,916	12,045	£12,776,416	£12,344,363	£22.73	£25.83	£3,566	384	392	400
51	West Cheshire College	560,289	4,165	4,300	3,689	12,865	£7,781,558	£7,029,411	£13.88	£15.11	£2,205	12	20	77
52	Chesterfield College	560,073	3,841	4,051	3,303	9,945	£10,218,762	£8,971,696	£18.24	£22.53	£2,445	194	323	157
53	Walsall College of Arts & Technology	560,000	4,212	4,345	3,524	9,048	£9,718,929	£9,454,211	£17.35	£19.32	£2,593	130	182	219
54	Plymouth College of Further Education	556,235	4,468	4,600	4,022	10,992	£10,273,124	£9,830,741	£18.46	£20.33	£2,502	206	240	179
55	Newham (Community) College of Further Education	552,592	5,036	4,835	3,944	13,260	£13,925,275	£13,274,809	£25.20	£26.68	£2,716	413	400	283
56	Doncaster College	547,849	4,582	4,875	4,069	15,759	£11,483,151	£11,246,965	£20.96	£26.48	£2,689	335	397	268

Comparison of Further Education Colleges Ordered Highest 94/95 Funding Units First

06-Sep-94

Count	College	94/95 Funding Units	93/4 Actual Wt FTE	93/94 Wt FTE Target	93/94 Target FTE	93/94 Target Students	94/95 Recurrent Grant	93/94 Recurrent Grant	ALF 94/95	ALF 93/94	Unit Cost 92/93	94/95 ALF Rank	93/94 ALF Rank	92/93 Unit Cost Rank
57	North Warwickshire College of Technology	540,225	4,498	4,322	3,646	11,335	£8,629,171	£8,265,489	£15.97	£17.01	£2,210	70	77	79
58	Northampton College	534,889	4,089	4,089	3,569	9,992	£8,206,167	£7,501,067	£15.34	£16.58	£2,040	47	63	42
59	Monkwearmouth College	532,699	3,881	3,770	3,322	10,585	£9,397,526	£8,550,979	£17.64	£18.96	£2,595	150	154	221
60	Norfolk College of Arts & Technology	530,538	3,997	4,131	3,541	8,986	£8,839,784	£8,549,114	£16.66	£18.41	£2,479	99	121	168
61	Halton College	530,527	4,118	4,103	3,582	10,899	£7,616,398	£6,432,769	£14.35	£14.77	£1,708	16	17	8
62	Colchester Institute	527,051	4,091	4,319	3,618	8,385	£9,574,920	£9,498,929	£18.16	£20.70	£2,634	190	255	244
63	Richmond Upon Thames	525,000	4,244	3,941	3,586	4,538	£11,273,112	£10,976,740	£21.47	£21.84	£2,679	355	304	262
64	Cornwall College	522,179	4,293	4,258	3,519	6,618	£9,682,104	£8,882,664	£18.54	£20.15	£2,492	213	229	175
65	Peterborough Regional College	521,846	3,972	3,833	3,307	10,639	£9,325,931	£8,627,133	£17.87	£19.10	£2,681	164	166	264
66	Guildford College of Further & Higher Education	521,213	4,062	4,202	3,539	6,453	£10,130,213	£10,326,415	£19.43	£21.25	£2,985	263	278	354
67	Chichester College of Arts & Technology	514,217	3,739	3,584	3,077	6,453	£7,827,240	£6,872,028	£15.22	£15.24	£2,167	40	24	70
68	North Tyneside College	512,008	3,322	3,347	2,842	7,241	£8,608,241	£7,067,521	£16.81	£18.59	£2,502	106	129	178
69	Grimsby College	510,754	3,819	3,815	3,148	10,786	£7,660,058	£7,066,474	£14.99	£15.60	£2,211	31	32	80
70	Hackney Community College	510,572	3,969	3,790	3,190	9,608	£14,833,815	£14,863,542	£29.05	£29.39	£3,760	424	415	408
71	North East Worcestershire College	506,057	3,846	4,029	3,468	9,369	£7,451,631	£7,370,555	£14.72	£16.62	£2,006	22	64	36
72	Reading College of Technology	504,846	3,624	3,696	3,089	8,294	£8,784,492	£8,350,278	£17.40	£20.00	£2,776	136	218	300
73	York College of Further & Higher Education	502,391	3,805	4,021	3,297	8,699	£7,896,847	£7,968,564	£15.71	£18.27	£2,519	54	118	187
74	Northbrook College, West Sussex	502,305	3,587	3,652	2,910	5,191	£8,007,453	£7,259,704	£15.94	£17.13	£2,546	67	80	201
75	Bridgwater College	502,024	2,913	2,682	2,333	5,384	£7,685,006	£5,630,041	£15.30	£14.99	£2,354	46	19	127
76	Kingsway College	501,059	3,258	3,273	2,917	10,203	£9,019,058	£8,705,654	£18.00	£20.11	£2,366	173	227	130
77	Mid-Warwickshire College	500,100	4,114	4,331	3,651	11,145	£7,892,098	£7,545,027	£15.78	£17.42	£1,973	57	87	52
78	North Hertfordshire College	500,016	3,686	3,676	3,236	12,798	£10,407,522	£10,183,485	£20.81	£23.69		328	364	437
79	Waltham Forest College	498,771	3,979	3,540	2,950	8,472	£10,434,143	£10,100,816	£20.92	£22.72	£2,822	333	332	322
80	Leicester South Fields College	497,831	3,907	3,653	2,809	7,306	£7,938,904	£6,392,032	£15.94	£16.14	£2,135	66	48	60
81	Tresham Institute	490,756	3,751	3,953	3,394	9,508	£8,828,965	£9,073,962	£17.99	£20.29	£2,687	172	238	267
82	Hammersmith & West London College	487,525	3,270	2,738	2,489	6,556	£10,379,066	£9,316,935	£21.28	£20.10	£3,259	348	224	384
83	Barnfield College	480,658	3,382	3,663	3,145	8,004	£6,937,978	£6,453,933	£14.43	£16.07	£1,486	17	43	1
84	Runshaw College	475,256	3,177	3,125	2,861	5,924	£6,676,909	£5,716,532	£14.04	£14.24	£1,979	13	13	31

Comparison of Further Education Colleges Ordered Highest 94/95 Funding Units First

06-Sep-94

Count	College	94/95 Funding Units	93/4 Actual Wt FTE	93/94 Wt FTE Target	93/94 Target FTE	93/94 Target Students	94/95 Recurrent Grant	93/94 Recurrent Grant	ALF 94/95	ALF 93/94	Unit Cost 92/93	94/95 ALF Rank	93/94 ALF Rank	92/93 Unit Cost Rank
85	Gateshead College	470,750	3,064	2,931	2,547	9,564	£7,840,843	£6,969,638	£16.65	£16.90	£2,765	98	74	298
86	Barnet College	470,438	3,065	3,140	2,635	7,780	£8,277,964	£7,093,371	£17.59	£17.58	£2,245	148	92	91
87	Bury College	469,885	4,025	4,365	3,859	7,868	£8,995,563	£9,331,497	£19.14	£21.87	£2,380	257	305	134
88	Hertford Regional College	469,856	3,714	3,408	2,808	6,293	£7,988,714	£7,396,957	£17.00	£16.89	£2,290	114	73	109
89	South Trafford College	465,324	3,176	3,044	2,746	8,848	£7,159,624	£5,773,890	£15.38	£16.53	£2,155	49	61	65
90	Derby Tertiary College, Wilmorton	464,547	3,276	3,825	3,380	9,701	£7,623,964	£8,067,687	£16.41	£19.43	£2,385	89	187	135
91	Southwark College	464,026	4,207	3,329	2,932	7,816	£10,915,704	£11,288,215	£23.52	£26.30	£2,715	396	395	281
92	Brooklands College	461,419	3,432	3,327	2,733	4,565	£8,392,322	£7,285,002	£18.18	£19.68	£2,443	191	198	154
93	Westminster College	461,110	4,123	4,016	3,895	13,178	£10,213,292	£9,964,187	£22.14	£21.73	£2,401	373	299	140
94	West Thames College	460,544	3,786	3,258	2,772	6,102	£9,858,315	£8,817,813	£21.40	£20.99		353	267	442
95	Basingstoke College of Technology	458,448	3,230	3,197	2,662	6,071	£8,065,113	£7,298,745	£17.59	£18.24	£2,578	147	116	215
96	St Austell College	457,462	3,479	3,609	3,165	5,977	£7,707,649	£7,038,949	£16.84	£19.06	£2,328	107	165	120
97	Rotherham College of Arts & Technology	456,526	3,566	3,636	3,033	10,555	£7,224,580	£6,841,458	£15.82	£16.86	£2,314	59	71	116
98	Brunel College of Arts & Technology	454,700	3,682	3,880	2,995	7,973	£10,214,915	£9,975,503	£22.46	£26.74	£2,855	377	402	328
99	Somerset College of Arts & Technology	454,689	3,115	3,426	3,046	7,747	£8,190,915	£8,435,546	£18.01	£21.04	£2,790	175	269	312
100	New College, Durham	449,802	3,366	3,339	2,847	9,579	£8,951,776	£7,831,825	£19.90	£20.68	£2,704	292	254	274
101	Accrington & Rossendale College	446,739	3,320	3,411	2,936	8,745	£7,761,029	£7,192,798	£17.37	£20.29	£2,449	131	237	160
102	Canterbury College	446,438	3,243	3,231	2,678	4,823	£6,783,554	£5,592,378	£15.19	£15.83	£2,216	39	37	84
103	Southampton Technical College	446,241	3,809	4,167	3,440	11,313	£9,438,333	£9,914,215	£21.15	£24.43	£2,787	343	374	306
104	Tameside College of Technology	445,094	4,290	4,122	3,576	10,844	£8,225,381	£7,841,164	£18.48	£19.64	£2,193	210	196	74
105	Farnborough College of Technology	440,351	3,120	3,170	2,780	8,640	£7,667,139	£7,636,593	£17.41	£18.92	£2,859	137	149	330
106	Barking College	432,972	3,026	2,950	2,378	5,342	£8,493,606	£7,749,641	£19.61	£19.14	£3,066	276	169	367
107	Stafford College	429,891	3,231	3,834	3,372	7,787	£7,434,660	£7,968,553	£17.29	£21.76	£2,392	126	300	138
108	Yeovil College	428,000	2,988	2,957	2,653	6,963	£7,492,023	£7,135,260	£17.50	£18.95	£2,732	144	153	286
109	Shrewsbury College of Arts & Technology	423,458	3,224	3,564	3,055	7,301	£7,768,041	£8,416,079	£18.34	£21.08	£2,664	200	270	257
110	Harlow College	421,531	3,667	4,536	3,910	11,474	£7,727,178	£7,933,448	£18.33	£20.03	£1,989	199	221	34
111	North Lindsey College	421,506	2,956	2,884	2,396	7,677	£6,108,394	£5,719,470	£14.49	£15.26	£2,348	19	25	125
112	South Cheshire College	420,169	3,651	3,781	3,262	10,748	£6,464,571	£5,969,133	£15.38	£17.07	£1,820	48	78	18

Spreadsheet Comparisons of all Colleges

Comparison of Further Education Colleges Ordered Highest 94/95 Funding Units First

06-Sep-94

Count	College	94/95 Funding Units	93/4 Actual Wt FTE	93/94 Wt FTE Target	93/94 Target FTE	93/94 Target Students	94/95 Recurrent Grant	93/94 Recurrent Grant	ALF 94/95	ALF 93/94	Unit Cost 92/93	94/95 ALF Rank	93/94 ALF Rank	92/93 Unit Cost Rank
113	North Lincolnshire College	418,299	3,301	3,081	2,681	6,434	£7,299,018	£7,255,485	£17.44	£19.40	£2,969	138	185	351
114	City of Westminster College	415,783	3,126	3,129	2,689	6,078	£9,856,677	£9,778,449	£23.70	£24.85	£3,058	397	381	366
115	Tower Hamlets College	414,564	3,348	2,945	2,641	4,803	£11,208,421	£10,808,506	£27.03	£26.78	£3,295	416	403	389
116	Salford College	414,150	3,447	3,326	2,878	9,684	£7,589,593	£7,053,525	£18.32	£18.76	£2,603	198	141	224
117	Hugh Baird College	413,525	3,240	3,444	2,773	5,491	£6,596,264	£6,096,362	£15.95	£16.64	£1,787	68	65	11
118	Southgate College	412,568	3,301	3,289	2,797	8,706	£7,688,024	£7,314,961	£18.63	£19.36	£2,216	221	183	85
119	Peoples College of Tertiary Education	410,880	2,651	3,987	3,136	7,540	£5,545,673	£6,100,850	£13.49	£22.69	£1,692	6	329	7
120	South Nottingham College	410,051	2,340	2,340	1,979	4,584	£6,248,799	£4,943,670	£15.23	£16.33	£2,273	42	53	102
121	Weymouth College	409,911	2,849	2,914	2,569	4,569	£7,248,364	£6,717,668	£17.68	£19.50	£2,574	152	190	211
122	South Birmingham College	409,387	3,127	2,687	2,259	6,325	£6,713,981	£4,900,716	£16.40	£15.28	£2,430	87	26	435
123	South Downs College	409,090	3,196	3,115	2,699	7,516	£7,296,285	£6,724,687	£17.83	£18.60	£2,274	161	131	152
124	Amersham & Wycombe College	408,913	3,544	3,480	3,027	4,629	£7,564,004	£7,224,455	£18.49	£20.06	£2,274	211	223	103
125	Crawley College	408,768	3,105	3,182	2,629	6,877	£6,872,111	£6,557,358	£16.81	£18.50	£2,594	104	124	220
126	Kingston College	405,313	2,970	2,975	2,528	5,504	£9,016,133	£8,594,979	£22.24	£23.39	£2,929	374	354	343
127	Worcester College of Technology	404,552	3,358	3,461	2,970	6,945	£6,461,878	£6,566,949	£15.97	£16.88	£2,092	71	72	52
128	Warrington Collegiate Institute	404,281					£6,782,831	£6,183,073	£16.77	£18.15		103	112	434
129	Mackworth College, Derby	399,109	3,909	3,901	3,362	7,133	£7,233,251	£7,098,382	£18.12	£18.93	£2,018	187	150	37
130	Calderdale College	397,821	2,847	2,834	2,453	6,976	£7,750,421	£6,710,321	£19.48	£22.19	£2,549	269	314	202
131	Bolton College	396,229	3,405	3,659	3,083	9,952	£7,789,889	£8,106,024	£19.66	£22.41	£2,789	283	316	308
132	Sutton Coldfield College of Further Education	395,460	4,117	4,020	3,473	8,313	£6,471,200	£6,076,244	£16.36	£17.09	£2,033	84	79	41
133	Knowsley Community College	395,190	4,022	4,063	3,572	8,454	£5,372,054	£4,852,804	£13.59	£14.19	£1,810	7	10	14
134	Weston-Super-Mare College	395,120	3,015	2,971	2,560	8,140	£6,238,629	£5,803,376	£15.78	£16.21	£2,210	56	51	78
135	Hendon College	394,575	3,273	3,040	2,755	9,257	£6,270,176	£5,593,377	£15.89	£15.20	£1,883	64	22	23
136	Fareham College	389,157	2,963	2,865	2,490	7,338	£6,750,643	£6,441,453	£17.34	£18.37	£2,441	128	119	153
137	Milton Keynes College	384,838	2,613	2,635	2,231	5,575	£5,761,521	£5,290,653	£14.97	£17.50	£2,254	30	88	93
138	Bexley College	383,686	3,501	3,397	2,771	6,086	£6,875,668	£6,307,952	£17.92	£18.26	£2,254	166	117	446
139	Epping Forest College	380,298	3,167	3,141	2,764	6,195	£6,435,157	£6,093,899	£16.92	£17.20	£2,112	112	82	54
140	Darlington College of Technology	379,605	2,994	3,065	2,488	8,338	£6,739,381	£6,449,168	£17.75	£18.92	£2,543	154	147	199

Comparison of Further Education Colleges Ordered Highest 94/95 Funding Units First

06-Sep-94

Count	College	94/95 Funding Units	93/4 Actual Wt FTE	93/94 Wt FTE Target	93/94 Target FTE	93/94 Target Students	94/95 Recurrent Grant	93/94 Recurrent Grant	ALF 94/95	ALF 93/94	Unit Cost 92/93	94/95 ALF Rank	93/94 ALF Rank	92/93 Unit Cost Rank
141	Hopwood Hall College	379,362	3,628	4,006	3,391	7,550	£10,926,592	£12,020,453	£28.80	£33.20	£3,443	423	423	395
142	North Devon College	378,736	2,892	2,998	2,570	4,956	£6,136,643	£5,745,920	£16.20	£17.89	£2,158	77	104	66
143	Thurrock College	378,474	2,601	2,720	2,191	5,170	£6,202,005	£5,617,758	£16.38	£17.25	£2,362	86	83	129
144	Harrogate College of Arts & Technology	378,271	2,820	3,098	2,602	8,954	£4,441,449	£4,233,984	£11.74	£13.25	£1,628	1	5	4
145	Salisbury College	373,785	2,427	2,478	2,109	5,754	£6,111,836	£5,561,270	£16.35	£17.00	£2,600	83	76	223
146	Henley College (The)	372,513	2,250	2,301	2,011	3,068	£5,438,515	£4,737,382	£14.60	£15.41	£2,172	20	28	71
147	Burton Upon Trent Technical College	371,600	2,949	2,962	2,487	7,122	£6,543,112	£6,364,895	£17.60	£18.22	£2,213	149	113	81
148	Thanet College	370,000	3,094	3,074	2,589	4,178	£6,140,305	£5,293,366	£16.59	£18.60	£2,045	94	130	43
149	Eastleigh College	369,092	2,522	2,501	2,209	6,285	£6,137,769	£5,757,757	£16.62	£17.80	£2,689	96	102	269
150	Wearside College	367,594	3,043	3,097	2,652	8,445	£6,655,139	£6,473,871	£18.10	£18.76	£2,781	184	140	304
151	Bedford College of Higher Education	362,724	3,127	3,380	2,806	8,713	£6,834,651	£7,067,891	£18.84	£21.47	£2,484	241	288	169
152	Charles Keene College of Further Education	360,000	3,127	3,340	2,825	7,945	£6,405,540	£6,610,464	£17.79	£20.24	£2,461	158	234	162
153	Brighton College of Technology	358,855	2,401	2,392	2,004	6,367	£7,320,420	£6,703,681	£20.39	£22.81	£3,235	314	336	382
154	North East Surrey College of Technology	356,347	2,971	3,281	2,693	5,579	£8,221,310	£8,746,074	£23.07	£27.95	£3,101	391	410	372
155	Nelson & Colne College	352,927	2,461	2,439	2,182	5,488	£5,241,985	£4,935,956	£14.85	£15.86	£2,268	25	39	98
156	City of Bath College	352,028	2,553	2,799	2,402	7,577	£6,326,726	£6,515,681	£17.97	£21.14	£2,751	171	274	293
157	West Nottinghamshire College	351,806	3,264	3,310	2,727	8,241	£6,531,754	£6,292,634	£18.56	£19.91	£2,126	215	213	57
158	Thomas Danby College	349,333	2,194	2,279	1,859	3,493	£5,596,263	£5,230,152	£16.02	£16.07	£2,629	74	44	238
159	Uxbridge College	347,525	2,748	2,792	2,406	5,601	£6,530,115	£6,102,911	£18.79	£20.22	£2,201	236	233	75
160	Longlands College of Further Education	347,409	2,588	2,406	1,866	6,782	£6,555,531	£5,391,062	£18.87	£19.91	£2,479	242	214	167
161	East Surrey College	343,137	2,729	2,682	2,229	3,860	£6,425,095	£6,219,840	£18.72	£19.91	£2,631	233	215	240
162	Tile Hill College of Further Education	342,646	2,568	2,499	2,112	5,180	£6,154,539	£5,698,647	£17.96	£19.24	£2,619	170	177	231
163	Kirby College of Further Education	342,508	2,171	2,044	1,946	6,917	£5,112,086	£4,643,130	£14.92	£15.71	£2,524	29	35	192
164	Yorkshire Coast College of Further & Higher Ed.	341,000	2,852	2,726	2,344	7,216	£4,931,260	£4,434,586	£14.46	£14.38	£1,980	18	15	32
165	Halesowen College	340,000	2,635	2,869	2,728	7,287	£6,350,394	£6,135,646	£18.67	£21.48	£2,281	225	289	105
166	Mid-Cheshire College of Further Education	339,455	2,862	2,927	2,378	7,176	£5,444,808	£4,963,362	£16.04	£17.75	£1,855	75	100	29
167	South East Derbyshire College	337,490	2,669	2,725	2,428	5,985	£6,155,446	£5,779,762	£18.23	£20.28	£2,425	193	236	150
168	Oldham College	332,668	2,853	2,988	2,437	4,952	£6,817,687	£6,697,139	£20.49	£22.91	£2,632	316	339	242

Comparison of Further Education Colleges Ordered Highest 94/95 Funding Units First

06-Sep-94

Count	College	94/95 Funding Units	93/4 Actual Wt FTE	93/4 Wt FTE Target	93/94 Target FTE	93/94 Target Students	94/95 Recurrent Grant	93/94 Recurrent Grant	ALF 94/95	ALF 93/94	Unit Cost 92/93	94/95 ALF Rank	93/94 ALF Rank	92/93 Unit Cost Rank
169	North West Kent College of Technology	330,683	2,412	2,273	1,971	3,799	£5,149,940	£4,614,642	£15.57	£15.98	£2,353	52	40	126
170	Cleveland Tertiary College	329,010	2,091	1,804	1,530	6,911	£5,806,702	£4,826,851	£17.64	£16.47	£2,272	151	57	101
171	Skelmersdale College	328,468	2,398	2,351	2,051	5,827	£4,381,961	£4,072,454	£13.34	£13.66	£1,823	4	7	19
172	Lancaster & Morecambe College	327,419	2,323	2,347	2,043	5,100	£5,082,424	£4,558,228	£15.52	£16.76	£2,285	50	67	107
173	Basford Hall College	326,972	2,814	3,064	2,471	5,983	£5,471,658	£5,566,285	£16.73	£19.06	£2,270	101	161	99
174	East Birmingham College	322,383	2,791	2,596	2,245	6,060	£4,926,216	£4,482,453	£15.28	£15.68	£2,134	44	34	59
175	North Nottinghamshire College	322,051	1,975	1,942	1,706	4,717	£5,598,101	£4,356,499	£17.38	£19.37	£2,617	134	184	228
176	Wulfrun College	322,000	3,841	3,463	2,965	11,788	£6,092,501	£5,769,414	£18.92	£19.64	£1,854	248	195	21
177	Southport College	321,435	3,015	3,015	2,629	8,104	£6,605,971	£5,724,412	£20.55	£24.64	£2,070	320	377	47
178	Coventry Technical College	321,031	2,508	2,244	1,755	5,891	£6,798,244	£5,865,612	£21.17	£22.81	£3,259	344	334	385
179	Chelmsford College	315,701	2,352	2,758	2,433	5,411	£5,329,087	£5,627,336	£16.88	£20.92	£2,346	110	263	124
180	West Suffolk College	315,188	2,000	1,785	1,531	3,609	£5,380,047	£4,290,309	£17.06	£18.01	£2,733	117	107	287
181	Burnley College	311,535	2,420	2,515	2,079	6,022	£5,057,134	£4,914,610	£16.23	£17.68	£2,252	78	97	92
182	Bournville College of Further Education	310,372	3,128	2,958	2,620	8,948	£5,342,905	£4,463,580	£17.21	£19.06	£1,820	123	164	17
183	North Trafford College of Further Education	305,000	2,435	2,514	2,039	9,484	£4,758,158	£4,401,626	£15.55	£16.40	£2,119	51	56	56
184	South Bristol College	304,833	2,163	2,159	1,841	6,819	£5,549,500	£5,305,449	£18.20	£21.28	£3,055	192	279	365
185	Airedale & Wharfdale College	304,773	1,817	1,640	1,478	5,281	£4,572,705	£4,257,640	£15.00	£14.23	£2,540	33	12	196
186	Basildon College	304,061	2,095	2,307	2,111	4,519	£4,817,127	£4,841,334	£15.84	£19.04	£2,328	60	160	119
187	Weald College	302,914	2,210	2,214	2,002	4,769	£5,030,331	£4,710,048	£16.60	£16.85	£2,088	95	70	51
188	Birmingham College of Food & Tourism	301,920	2,156	2,109	1,820	4,249	£4,740,850	£4,282,611	£15.70	£16.48	£2,562	53	58	206
189	Hastings College of Arts & Technology	298,764	2,118	2,070	1,702	4,594	£5,813,797	£5,638,998	£19.45	£20.82	£3,099	265	257	371
190	Stourbridge College	297,015	2,227	2,101	1,757	5,620	£5,353,528	£4,651,197	£18.02	£18.50	£2,485	177	126	171
191	Newcastle-Under-Lyme College	296,672	2,168	2,232	2,044	4,948	£4,676,518	£4,667,184	£15.76	£17.37	£2,257	55	85	95
192	Merton College	295,985	2,232	2,482	2,109	5,570	£5,170,858	£5,276,386	£17.47	£19.89	£2,181	141	211	72
193	Trowbridge College	294,354	2,209	2,238	1,904	6,112	£5,420,341	£5,196,875	£18.41	£20.51	£2,712	203	246	280
194	Carlisle College	294,319	2,353	2,371	2,021	5,221	£5,317,158	£5,102,839	£18.06	£19.44	£2,591	182	189	218
195	Herefordshire College of Technology	289,142	2,533	2,456	2,106	7,066	£5,024,394	£5,009,366	£17.37	£19.68	£2,308	132	199	114
196	Lewes Tertiary College	288,641	2,013	1,987	1,817	3,719	£5,460,903	£4,773,517	£18.91	£20.86	£2,711	247	261	278

Comparison of Further Education Colleges Ordered Highest 94/95 Funding Units First

06-Sep-94

Count	College	94/95 Funding Units	93/4 Actual Wt FTE	93/94 Wt FTE Target	93/94 Target FTE	93/94 Target Students	94/95 Recurrent Grant	93/94 Recurrent Grant	ALF 94/95	ALF 93/94	Unit Cost 92/93	94/95 ALF Rank	93/94 ALF Rank	92/93 Unit Cost Rank
197	Soundwell College	287,204	1,944	2,196	1,947	6,641	£4,038,292	£3,824,140	£14.06	£16.57	£2,164	14	62	68
198	Filton College	286,000	2,109	1,902	1,715	4,856	£5,399,666	£4,774,240	£18.88	£19.53	£3,004	244	191	356
199	Stockton & Billingham College of Further Education	285,075	2,563	2,641	2,165	5,266	£4,852,411	£4,706,509	£17.02	£18.43	£1,981	115	122	33
200	Greenhill College, Harrow	283,961	2,471	2,581	2,379	8,253	£5,064,015	£4,859,899	£17.83	£19.06	£1,673	160	163	6
201	Loughborough College	280,016	2,086	2,195	1,899	4,701	£5,434,256	£5,036,382	£19.40	£24.15	£2,753	259	369	294
202	Rother Valley College	278,989	2,039	1,957	1,644	6,452	£3,446,178	£3,049,715	£12.35	£11.66	£1,755	2	2	10
203	Northumberland College of Arts & Technology	276,558	2,480	2,550	2,132	5,423	£5,083,591	£5,053,271	£18.38	£20.49	£2,622	202	245	234
204	Woolwich College	276,327	2,008	1,749	1,522	3,462	£6,238,317	£5,584,885	£22.57	£23.17	£3,138	383	347	375
205	Brockenhurst College	273,321	2,033	1,989	1,872	3,845	£4,671,791	£4,531,320	£17.09	£18.12	£2,472	120	110	164
206	Isle of Wight College (The)	272,743	1,954	1,978	1,657	4,866	£4,484,467	£4,400,851	£16.44	£18.92	£2,574	91	148	212
207	Dunstable College	270,000	2,030	2,123	1,783	4,458	£4,071,759	£3,866,818	£15.08	£16.75	£2,521	35	66	188
208	Telford College of Arts & Technology	268,984	2,265	2,301	2,033	7,576	£4,541,907	£4,413,904	£16.89	£18.50	£2,290	111	125	110
209	North Derbyshire Tertiary College	267,523	1,811	2,128	1,796	4,558	£4,514,973	£4,966,967	£16.87	£26.50	£2,704	109	398	275
210	Chippenham College	262,109	2,147	2,157	1,889	6,450	£4,186,126	£3,861,740	£15.97	£17.57	£1,947	72	90	25
211	Eastbourne College of Arts & Technology	261,645	2,185	2,201	1,862	4,289	£5,892,159	£5,810,808	£22.52	£26.95	£2,870	381	405	332
212	Peterlee College	257,971	1,948	2,000	1,735	4,729	£3,949,266	£3,834,239	£15.30	£16.20	£2,148	45	49	62
213	Enfield College	255,746	1,985	1,831	1,626	4,888	£4,471,410	£3,815,196	£17.48	£16.37	£2,190	142	55	73
214	Henley College, Coventry	255,739	1,759	1,604	1,415	6,116	£5,018,847	£4,364,215	£19.62	£20.20	£3,360	280	232	393
215	Stanmore College	250,685					£4,315,872	£3,895,191	£17.21	£17.65		124	94	433
216	Sixth Form College, Colchester (The)	249,457	1,843	1,864	1,772	1,772	£4,698,239	£4,504,544	£18.83	£20.10	£2,423	240	225	149
217	Barton Peveril College	249,043	1,780	1,677	1,515	1,515	£4,366,844	£4,013,643	£17.53	£17.26	£2,280	145	84	104
218	Cricklade College	248,724	1,742	1,752	1,573	3,759	£4,065,255	£3,842,396	£16.34	£17.83	£2,511	82	103	182
219	Braintree College	247,630	1,703	1,953	1,758	3,249	£4,562,765	£4,922,077	£18.42	£23.00	£0	205	344	426
220	Abingdon College	246,937	1,586	1,506	1,304	4,174	£3,902,840	£3,313,107	£15.80	£15.61	£2,514	58	33	185
221	High Peak College	246,575	1,735	1,658	1,499	3,594	£4,405,111	£4,361,496	£17.66	£18.85	£2,741	162	143	289
222	South East Essex Sixth Form College	245,394	1,747	1,825	1,756	1,756	£4,620,357	£4,543,124	£18.82	£20.32	£2,514	238	239	184
223	East Warwickshire College	244,923	2,028	1,971	1,705	6,244	£4,279,074	£4,199,288	£17.47	£18.67	£2,539	140	137	195
224	Lowestoft College	244,320	2,577	2,753	2,411	6,439	£4,955,320	£5,172,568	£20.28	£22.92	£2,139	306	340	61

Comparison of Further Education Colleges Ordered Highest 94/95 Funding Units First

06-Sep-94

Count	College	94/95 Funding Units	93/4 Actual Wt FTE	93/94 Wt FTE Target	93/94 Target FTE	93/94 Target Students	94/95 Recurrent Grant	93/94 Recurrent Grant	ALF 94/95	ALF 93/94	Unit Cost 92/93	94/95 ALF Rank	93/94 ALF Rank	92/93 Unit Cost Rank
225	Hartlepool College of Further Education	243,466	1,877	1,674	1,446	5,184	£4,408,262	£4,162,665	18.10	£19.13	£2,779	183	168	302
226	North Oxfordshire College	243,300	1,727	1,678	1,437	3,410	£4,222,133	£3,986,906	17.35	£18.67	£2,704	129	136	276
227	Ridge College (The)	243,106	1,667	1,489	1,415	1,415	£4,252,071	£4,164,614	17.49	£19.26	£0	143	180	429
228	Broxtowe College, Nottingham	242,418	2,177	2,177	2,012	6,845	£3,694,488	£3,361,682	15.24	£16.08	£1,831	43	46	20
229	Stroud College of Further Education	242,076	1,853	1,736	1,479	5,123	£4,543,480	£4,274,205	18.76	£18.87	£3,010	235	144	359
230	Luton Sixth Form College	241,407	1,699	1,662	1,575	1,718	£5,065,135	£4,908,077	20.98	£21.58	£2,961	338	297	350
231	Solihull Sixth Form College	239,300	1,717	1,714	1,620	1,620	£4,323,636	£4,141,414	18.06	£18.65	£2,406	181	135	143
232	Tamworth College	238,093	1,759	1,732	1,459	3,592	£3,486,328	£2,942,049	14.64	£14.39	£2,031	21	16	40
233	Boston College	237,056	1,959	1,961	1,640	3,879	£4,639,762	£4,248,866	19.57	£21.45	£2,504	273	287	180
234	Bromley College of Further & Higher Education	236,378	2,210	1,934	1,598	4,162	£4,975,017	£4,344,993	21.04	£21.14	£2,664	340	273	258
235	Leeds College of Technology	235,676	2,169	2,163	1,559	4,455	£5,300,390	£5,232,369	22.49	£23.95	£0	380	367	438
236	Alton College	226,550	1,587	1,546	1,425	2,708	£3,737,062	£3,255,280	16.49	£17.63	£2,241	93	93	90
237	Peter Symonds College	219,390	1,618	1,543	1,483	3,270	£4,132,930	£3,858,945	18.83	£18.73	£2,551	239	139	204
238	Newham Sixth Form College	217,329	1,616	1,619	1,350	1,350	£4,728,419	£4,452,372	21.75	£21.87	£0	364	306	430
239	Derwentside College	215,962	1,732	1,702	1,514	4,238	£3,870,944	£3,617,705	17.92	£19.69	£2,293	165	200	112
240	Cannock Chase Technical College	215,674	2,572	2,109	1,718	5,169	£3,258,219	£3,584,399	15.10	£21.80	£1,737	36	302	9
241	Queen Mary's College	215,569	1,543	1,614	1,562	1,562	£4,227,743	£4,104,605	19.61	£21.39	£2,574	279	284	213
242	Stoke-On-Trent Sixth Form College (City)	214,985	1,604	1,548	1,548	1,548	£4,023,334	£4,080,460	18.71	£19.97	£2,624	231	216	236
243	Bracknell College	214,231	1,721	1,946	1,773	6,400	£4,430,233	£4,648,723	20.68	£24.67	£2,844	325	378	324
244	Newark & Sherwood College	211,579	1,560	1,672	1,418	3,477	£3,115,644	£2,863,643	14.72	£16.34	£2,029	23	54	39
245	Godalming College	208,844	1,351	1,321	1,266	1,266	£3,860,257	£3,324,941	18.48	£19.01	£2,522	208	157	190
246	Macclesfield College of Further Education	207,928	1,851	1,822	1,680	7,899	£3,415,910	£3,309,990	16.42	£17.58	£2,064	90	91	46
247	Keighley College	205,056	2,174	1,903	1,587	6,104	£4,260,712	£4,092,903	20.77	£21.36	£2,422	327	282	148
248	Arnold & Carlton College	204,734	2,052	1,815	1,574	4,527	£3,976,909	£3,522,506	19.42	£19.85	£2,327	261	209	118
249	North Birmingham College	204,006	1,982	2,060	1,692	4,871	£4,514,029	£4,374,059	22.12	£27.51		371	406	445
250	Havering Sixth Form College	203,615	1,427	1,433	1,425	1,425	£4,140,649	£3,855,353	20.33	£21.00	£0	309	268	432
251	Stamford College	201,939	1,647	1,632	1,441	2,386	£3,308,355	£3,007,595	16.38	£17.50	£2,027	85	89	38
252	Selby College	201,530	1,195	1,184	1,029	2,524	£3,057,833	£2,428,779	15.17	£16.01	£2,691	37	41	270

Comparison of Further Education Colleges Ordered Highest 94/95 Funding Units First

06-Sep-94

Count	College	94/95 Funding Units	93/4 Actual Wt FTE	93/94 Wt FTE Target	93/94 Target FTE	93/94 Target Students	94/95 Recurrent Grant	93/94 Recurrent Grant	ALF 94/95	ALF 93/94	Unit Cost 92/93	94/95 ALF Rank	93/94 ALF Rank	92/93 Unit Cost Rank
253	Great Yarmouth College of Further Education	200,937	1,383	1,486	1,332	2,782	£3,563,697	£3,352,490	£17.73	£21.21	£2,516	153	276	186
254	Carshalton College	199,659	1,624	1,566	1,319	3,158	£4,289,965	£4,128,936	£21.48	£22.51	£2,583	356	322	216
255	Newbury College	199,331	1,705	1,707	1,457	5,112	£4,275,631	£4,127,057	£21.45	£23.49	£2,857	354	356	329
256	John Legott Sixth Form College	199,102	1,355	1,331	1,271	1,272	£3,865,701	£3,536,780	£19.41	£20.54		260	248	443
257	Wyggeston & Queen Elizabeth I College	197,885	1,235	1,216	1,126	1,126	£3,701,621	£3,252,743	£18.70	£19.75	£2,679	229	205	261
258	Isle College	196,152	1,538	1,677	1,393	1,977	£3,304,791	£3,372,236	£16.84	£19.72	£2,159	108	203	67
259	Sixth Form College, Farnborough (The)	194,000	1,388	1,390	1,327	1,396	£3,583,112	£3,361,268	£18.47	£19.17	£2,446	207	171	158
260	Strode College	193,884	1,424	1,424	1,275	2,830	£3,943,117	£3,798,764	£20.33	£22.03	£2,854	310	313	327
261	Palmers (Sixth Form) College	193,649	1,315	1,386	1,304	1,304	£3,605,422	£3,427,207	£18.61	£20.15	£2,488	220	228	172
262	Grantham College	193,340	1,455	1,402	1,223	3,512	£3,453,122	£3,276,207	£17.86	£19.00	£2,738	163	156	288
263	East Devon College	191,741	1,464	1,519	1,347	2,684	£3,558,336	£3,382,449	£18.55	£22.21	£2,527	214	315	194
264	Kensington & Chelsea College	189,618	1,448	1,311	1,108	4,688	£3,232,364	£2,488,348	£17.08	£15.34	£1,815	118	27	15
265	Orpington College of Further Education	189,218	1,421	1,360	1,294	2,140	£2,873,407	£2,663,028	£15.18	£14.35	£1,819	38	14	16
266	Redbridge College	187,358	1,835	1,782	1,546	4,673	£3,680,435	£3,698,930	£18.64	£21.48	£2,216	223	290	83
267	Royal Forest of Dean College	186,207	1,274	1,300	1,162	2,714	£3,477,882	£3,413,034	£18.67	£20.10	£3,024	226	226	361
268	Furness College	185,191	1,708	1,836	1,524	4,056	£3,322,151	£3,553,103	£17.93	£20.85	£2,255	167	258	94
269	New College, Swindon	184,795	1,360	1,258	1,189	1,411	£3,015,952	£2,839,879	£16.32	£16.07	£2,342	81	45	123
270	West Cumbria College	183,303	1,778	1,703	1,420	4,447	£4,054,832	£4,026,645	£22.12	£23.96	£2,404	372	368	141
271	Truro College	182,335	988	887	833	1,731	£3,357,909	£2,502,168	£18.41	£19.18	£0	204	173	427
272	Stratford Upon Avon College	181,011	1,559	1,500	1,383	3,649	£3,552,381	£3,370,380	£19.62	£22.02		281	312	441
273	Oldham Sixth Form College	181,008	1,218	1,226	1,150	1,150	£3,446,981	£3,224,491	£19.04	£20.01	£0	254	219	428
274	West Oxfordshire College	176,782	1,275	1,400	1,146	2,884	£2,803,707	£2,829,170	£15.86	£18.12	£2,395	61	109	139
275	Xaverian College	174,381	1,274	1,254	1,194	1,194	£3,448,068	£3,363,969	£19.77	£20.51	£2,645	288	247	251
276	Long Road Sixth Form College	174,132	1,123	1,066	1,027	1,027	£3,416,140	£2,934,828	£19.61	£20.03	£2,789	278	220	311
277	Huntingdonshire Regional College	173,474	1,472	1,569	1,365	4,217	£3,391,550	£3,214,739	£19.55	£23.04	£2,331	270	345	121
278	Kidderminster College	171,899	1,518	1,581	1,377	4,653	£2,956,850	£2,930,476	£17.20	£18.65	£2,215	122	133	82
279	Leyton Sixth Form College	171,047	1,049	945	900	900	£3,382,944	£2,869,333	£19.77	£19.14	£2,625	287	170	237
280	St Vincent College	170,275	1,088	1,105	1,081	1,617	£3,074,512	£2,752,473	£18.05	£18.71	£2,521	180	138	189

Comparison of Further Education Colleges Ordered Highest 94/95 Funding Units First

06-Sep-94

Count	College	94/95 Funding Units	93/4 Actual Wt FTE	93/94 Wt FTE Target	93/94 Target FTE	93/94 Target Students	94/95 Recurrent Grant	93/94 Recurrent Grant	ALF 94/95	ALF 93/94	Unit Cost 92/93	94/95 ALF Rank	93/94 ALF Rank	92/93 Unit Cost Rank
281	John Ruskin College	167,049	1,013	995	945	945	£3,616,917	£3,109,989	£21.65	£23.06	£2,780	362	346	303
282	Hills Road Sixth Form College	165,824	1,122	1,014	936	938	£3,153,263	£2,711,318	£19.01	£18.65	£2,707	253	134	277
283	Esher College	165,075	1,025	1,004	976	976	£2,833,431	£2,611,457	£17.16	£17.14	£2,611	121	81	226
284	East Yorkshire College of Further Education	165,000	1,131	1,148	969	2,751	£2,624,495	£2,494,767	£15.90	£16.22	£2,934	65	52	344
285	Havant College	164,500	1,180	1,149	1,092	1,092	£2,979,292	£2,829,337	£18.11	£18.23	£2,489	185	114	173
286	Winstanley College	162,750	1,122	1,118	1,059	1,062	£3,253,993	£2,944,790	£19.99	£21.55	£2,643	299	294	250
287	Worcester Sixth Form College	161,202	1,064	1,084	1,049	1,049	£2,802,221	£2,510,951	£17.38	£17.66	£2,271	133	96	100
288	Coalville Technical College	159,160	1,238	1,340	1,091	3,314	£2,957,173	£3,054,931	£18.58	£21.39	£2,944	217	283	347
289	Evesham College	152,494	1,173	1,134	1,020	3,027	£2,287,601	£2,073,981	£15.00	£15.46	£2,095	32	29	53
290	Daventry Tertiary College	151,527	1,168	1,174	1,091	2,558	£2,645,529	£2,383,359	£17.45	£18.90	£2,118	139	145	55
291	Coulsdon College	151,018	1,017	918	856	856	£2,955,761	£2,595,049	£19.57	£18.39	£3,197	272	120	444
292	High Pavement Sixth Form College	150,902	1,022	1,008	968	968	£2,858,315	£2,724,800	£18.94	£19.43	£2,716	249	188	282
293	Penwith College	150,219	1,155	1,102	1,054	1,899	£2,286,679	£1,978,096	£15.22	£15.75	£1,990	41	36	35
294	Sir George Monoux College	150,022	968	956	917	917	£2,969,188	£2,877,120	£19.79	£19.77	£2,634	289	206	243
295	Joseph Chamberlain Sixth Form College	149,909	1,193	1,257	1,214	1,375	£3,043,191	£3,114,952	£20.30	£21.96	£2,513	308	309	183
296	Taunton's College	147,796	1,275	1,119	1,065	1,065	£2,977,235	£2,974,771	£20.59	£23.63	£2,670	321	361	259
297	Lincolnshire College of Agriculture & Horticulture	147,317	1,055	1,161	838	1,662	£2,344,630	£2,711,507	£20.21	£22.43	£2,631	304	318	239
298	Norton Radstock College	146,648	1,056	970	833	4,171	£2,728,439	£1,660,503	£15.98	£14.22	£1,956	73	11	26
299	Cadbury Sixth Form College	146,063	1,056	1,092	1,032	1,032	£2,881,800	£2,641,277	£18.68	£19.81	£2,447	227	207	159
300	York Sixth Form College	144,345	936	951	915	915	£2,533,497	£2,741,960	£19.96	£21.24	£2,817	296	277	319
301	North Shropshire College (The)	144,095	1,179	1,297	1,146	4,114	£3,004,156	£2,810,249	£17.58	£20.86	£2,221	146	260	87
302	Greenhead College	144,037	1,040	1,016	946	946	£2,591,977	£2,817,366	£20.85	£21.80	£2,637	330	303	246
303	Hinckley College	143,896	1,315	1,405	1,235	3,868	£2,286,181	£1,929,267	£18.01	£23.57	£2,361	176	359	128
304	Joseph Priestley College	143,236	1,002	977	925	5,499	£2,605,215	£2,694,121	£15.96	£16.21	£2,218	69	50	86
305	Melton Mowbray College of Further Education	142,237	1,149	1,298	1,113	2,387	£2,915,502	£2,861,140	£18.31	£21.89	£2,410	196	307	146
306	St Brendan's Sixth Form College	142,157	980	976	943	990	£2,815,002	£2,625,935	£20.50	£21.53	£2,917	318	293	340
307	Queen Elizabeth Sixth Form College	141,237	982	950	899	911	£2,625,935	£2,501,846	£19.93	£20.47	£2,788	295	244	307
308	Carmel College	140,864	953	933	896	896	£2,501,846	£2,362,461	£17.76	£18.14	£2,565	156	111	208

Comparison of Further Education Colleges Ordered Highest 94/95 Funding Units First

06-Sep-94

Count	College	94/95 Funding Units	93/4 Actual Wt FTE	93/3/4 Wt FTE Target	93/4 Target FTE	92/93 Target Students	94/95 Recurrent Grant	93/94 Recurrent Grant	ALF 94/95	ALF 93/94	Unit Cost 92/93	94/95 ALF Rank	93/94 ALF Rank	92/93 Unit Cost Rank
309	Totton (Sixth Form) College	140,251	967	958	932	2,070	£2,601,071	£2,503,437	£18.54	£19.65	£2,655	212	197	254
310	Blackpool Sixth Form College (The)	140,000	1,058	1,035	998	998	£3,136,722	£3,096,468	£22.40	£23.66	£2,937	375	363	346
311	Craven College	139,771	1,051	1,040	949	2,764	£1,922,815	£1,726,046	£13.75	£14.07	£2,076	10	9	48
312	Leeds College of Building	139,631	931	928	667	2,328	£2,605,362	£2,396,837	£18.65	£20.59	£3,623	224	249	402
313	Worthing Sixth Form College	139,036	975	1,002	948	948	£2,652,898	£2,521,766	£19.08	£20.91	£2,550	255	262	203
314	Tynemouth College	138,519	1,001	892	851	860	£2,855,875	£2,620,069	£20.61	£20.45	£2,944	323	243	348
315	Bexhill College	137,591	962	967	950	982	£2,574,182	£2,433,064	£18.70	£19.74	£2,497	230	204	177
316	Richard Huish College (The)	136,761	928	875	825	825	£2,595,365	£2,286,665	£18.97	£19.40	£2,647	251	186	252
317	Wigston College of Further Education	136,580	898	965	869	2,179	£2,356,600	£2,402,243	£17.25	£18.95	£2,954	125	152	349
318	Holy Cross College	136,276	959	934	870	870	£2,324,531	£2,130,643	£17.05	£16.85	£2,205	116	69	76
319	Portsmouth (Sixth Form) College	135,643	1,018	962	903	1,132	£2,730,690	£2,528,417	£20.13	£20.19	£2,674	300	231	260
320	Reigate College	135,529	941	926	896	896	£2,549,150	£2,411,684	£18.80	£18.61	£2,590	237	132	217
321	Rockingham College of Further Education	135,025	1,024	877	819	2,570	£2,433,651	£2,036,528	£18.02	£15.17	£2,799	178	21	316
322	Itchen College	134,770	995	992	953	1,395	£2,675,481	£2,548,077	£19.85	£20.97	£2,623	290	265	235
323	Priestley College	134,767	987	956	897	897	£2,519,738	£2,374,871	£18.69	£19.17	£2,476	228	172	166
324	Cardinal Newman College	134,616	895	903	853	853	£2,871,029	£2,773,941	£21.32	£22.90	£3,137	351	338	374
325	Josiah Mason Sixth Form College	133,746	1,313	1,160	1,084	1,084	£3,052,240	£3,001,219	£22.82	£23.93	£2,642	387	366	249
326	Sir John Deane's College	133,625	935	888	850	850	£2,600,574	£2,448,751	£19.46	£19.26	£2,693	267	179	271
327	Beverley College of Further Education	133,524	1,083	1,060	912	2,850	£1,984,192	£1,844,045	£14.86	£15.86	£2,153	26	38	64
328	St Francis Xavier Sixth Form College	132,252	1,005	966	894	894	£3,356,528	£3,265,105	£25.38	£24.35	£2,881	414	371	334
329	North Area College	130,744	1,135	774	757	912	£2,613,736	£2,085,982	£19.99	£16.11	£2,789	298	47	309
330	Haywards Heath College	130,389	1,039	1,027	979	979	£2,929,857	£2,992,704	£22.47	£23.21	£2,819	378	348	335
331	Wyke Sixth Form College	130,056	989	1,087	1,040	1,065	£2,799,549	£3,023,271	£21.52	£25.34	£2,819	359	388	320
332	Sparsholt College, Hampshire	129,899	1,186	1,252	905	1,356	£3,730,967	£4,033,478	£28.72	£31.97	£3,612	422	421	401
333	King Edward VI College, Stourbridge	129,806	931	942	866	866	£2,763,788	£2,678,089	£21.29	£22.66	£2,703	350	327	273
334	St.John Rigby RC Sixth Form College	129,602	932	911	891	891	£2,583,536	£2,503,426	£19.93	£20.68	£2,795	294	253	313
335	College of Richard Collyer in Horsham (The)	129,355	932	905	866	866	£2,549,819	£2,334,999	£19.71	£20.65	£2,621	284	252	232
336	Cirencester College	127,928	965	946	889	1,948	£2,323,871	£2,141,817	£18.16	£18.50	£2,445	189	123	156

Comparison of Further Education Colleges Ordered Highest 94/95 Funding Units First

06-Sep-94

Count	College	94/95 Funding Units	93/4 Actual Wt FTE	93/94 Wt FTE Target	93/94 Target FTE	93/94 Target Students	94/95 Recurrent Grant	93/94 Recurrent Grant	ALF 94/95	ALF 93/94	Unit Cost 92/93	94/95 ALF Rank	93/94 ALF Rank	92/93 Unit Cost Rank
337	Bishop Burton College	127,750	1,114	1,103	788	1,835	£2,881,777	£2,787,018	£22.55	£24.82	£3,558	382	380	399
338	Rowley Regis College	127,256	940	821	805	847	£2,782,580	£2,548,150	£21.86	£20.78	£3,169	367	256	379
339	Bishop Auckland College	126,864	986	1,005	839	3,111	£2,360,102	£2,325,224	£18.60	£19.85	£2,637	219	210	245
340	Aquinas College	125,128	855	815	783	783	£2,430,063	£2,239,689	£19.42	£19.71	£2,711	262	201	279
341	West Sussex College of Agriculture & Horticulture	124,816	856	813	581	1,094	£2,172,323	£1,683,971	£17.40	£18.93	£2,323	135	151	117
342	St Phillip's RC Sixth Form College	124,249	965	968	922	922	£2,635,139	£2,451,292	£21.20	£22.87	£2,523	345	337	191
343	Thomas Rotherham College	122,951	838	836	779	779	£2,255,449	£2,074,930	£18.34	£18.90	£2,408	201	146	144
344	Ashton-Under-Lyne Sixth Form College	122,018	877	835	787	810	£2,391,526	£2,131,485	£19.60	£19.99	£2,390	275	217	137
345	Birkenhead Sixth Form College	121,646	905	873	840	840	£2,266,384	£2,154,357	£18.63	£19.06	£2,456	222	162	161
346	New College, Telford	120,483	901	991	920	920	£2,769,462	£2,924,458	£22.98	£24.98	£2,893	389	364	338
347	Hereford Sixth Form College	120,080	886	894	848	848	£2,219,818	£2,163,565	£18.48	£18.97	£2,367	209	155	131
348	Otley College of Agriculture & Horticulture	120,040	997	958	705	1,943	£2,131,650	£2,018,608	£17.75	£19.10	£2,262	155	167	97
349	King George V College	120,000	815	789	731	731	£2,227,660	£1,974,876	£18.56	£19.02	£2,542	216	159	198
350	Huddersfield New College	119,345	856	912	861	861	£2,599,477	£2,727,678	£21.78	£23.64	£2,929	365	362	342
351	Shena Simon College	118,816	877	990	942	942	£2,528,474	£2,658,753	£21.28	£24.54	£2,729	346	376	285
352	Varndean College	118,372	791	789	777	777	£2,242,112	£2,077,954	£18.94	£19.81	£2,618	250	208	230
353	Brighton, Hove & Sussex Sixth Form College	115,975	883	949	906	927	£2,400,496	£2,503,124	£20.69	£22.43	£2,612	326	319	227
354	Reaseheath College	114,434	938	964	688	1,448	£2,391,848	£2,262,865	£20.90	£22.41	£2,782	332	317	305
355	Stockton Sixth Form College	113,857	859	843	795	795	£2,248,830	£2,187,578	£19.75	£20.95	£2,632	286	264	241
356	Kendal College	113,064	799	753	663	1,579	£2,244,609	£1,887,812	£19.85	£22.46	£3,043	291	320	363
357	Bicton College of Agriculture	112,973	802	996	760	972	£2,293,213	£2,184,012	£20.29	£26.81	£2,761	307	404	297
358	Lincolnshire College of Art & Design	111,621	1,055	979	702	1,542	£2,172,697	£2,087,125	£19.46	£20.86	£2,166	266	259	69
359	Christ the King Sixth Form College	111,000	696	714	690	690	£2,312,113	£2,134,915	£20.83	£21.20	£0	329	275	424
360	Woodhouse (Sixth Form) College	110,874	698	717	664	664	£2,154,262	£2,043,892	£19.43	£19.31	£2,541	264	181	197
361	New College, Pontefract	110,793	796	797	752	766	£2,329,255	£2,170,788	£21.02	£22.71	£2,745	339	330	291
362	Shrewsbury Sixth Form College	110,784	739	721	697	697	£2,239,309	£2,096,731	£20.21	£20.98	£2,883	303	266	336
363	Leek College of Further Education & Science	110,036	880	856	758	2,020	£1,975,378	£1,823,987	£17.95	£19.21	£2,232	168	174	89
364	Wilberforce Sixth Form College	109,973	777	873	854	854	£2,190,867	£2,410,195	£19.92	£22.92	£2,797	293	341	314

Comparison of Further Education Colleges Ordered Highest 94/95 Funding Units First

06-Sep-94

Count	College	94/95 Funding Units	93/4 Actual Wt FTE	93/94 Wt FTE Target	93/94 Target FTE	93/94 Target Students	94/95 Recurrent Grant	93/94 Recurrent Grant	ALF 94/95	ALF 93/94	Unit Cost 92/93	94/95 ALF Rank	93/94 ALF Rank	92/93 Unit Cost Rank
365	Widnes Sixth Form College	109,870	738	749	725	725	£2,239,983	£2,135,351	£20.38	£21.42	£2,823	313	286	323
366	Scarborough Sixth Form College	108,698	824	813	767	767	£2,222,377	£2,174,537	£20.44	£21.40	£2,618	315	285	229
367	Barrow-In-Furness Sixth Form College	107,105	784	775	745	745	£2,096,260	£2,005,990	£19.57	£20.64	£2,546	271	251	200
368	Strode's College	106,893	776	764	747	770	£2,081,972	£2,011,567	£19.47	£19.55	£2,596	268	192	222
369	Gateway Sixth Form College	106,612	860	876	841	931	£2,423,429	£2,490,677	£22.73	£24.42	£2,819	385	372	321
370	Shipley College	106,159	848	811	720	2,332	£2,333,198	£2,291,943	£21.97	£23.39	£3,389	368	355	394
371	Newton Rigg College	105,708	774	669	492	1,365	£2,213,059	£1,909,456	£20.93	£23.59	£3,008	334	360	357
372	St Charles Catholic Sixth Form College	103,766	747	678	671	671	£2,606,610	£2,585,923	£25.12	£22.68	£3,248	412	328	383
373	Leeds College of Art & Design	103,591	811	799	571	749	£1,966,778	£1,691,125	£18.98	£20.16		252	230	439
374	North Bolton Sixth Form College	103,571	795	767	653	653	£1,895,298	£1,810,218	£18.30	£18.09	£2,379	195	108	133
375	Hartpury College	103,230	776	768	549	790	£1,891,218	£1,676,612	£18.32	£20.39	£2,664	197	241	256
376	Franklin Sixth Form College	103,023	875	870	834	834	£2,422,758	£2,320,649	£23.51	£25.48	£2,695	395	389	272
377	Pendleton College	101,466	821	820	792	792	£2,146,091	£2,201,119	£21.15	£21.55	£2,721	342	295	284
378	Loreto College	100,581	825	927	889	898	£2,580,422	£2,774,647	£25.65	£30.88	£3,049	415	417	364
379	Portsmouth College of Art & Design	98,252	835	862	673	1,354	£2,147,308	£2,186,668	£21.85	£25.94	£2,801	366	393	317
380	Eccles College	98,245	747	780	748	748	£2,032,264	£1,965,439	£20.68	£22.79	£2,553	324	333	205
381	Bournemouth & Poole College of Art & Design	97,849	912	930	664	737	£2,394,884	£2,213,386	£24.47	£27.78	£3,008	409	408	358
382	King Edward VI College, Nuneaton	97,576	727	721	676	677	£1,825,629	£1,735,389	£18.71	£19.02	£2,390	232	158	136
383	Bilborough Sixth Form College	94,586	692	708	676	676	£2,082,142	£1,945,927	£22.01	£24.45	£2,756	369	375	295
384	Ludlow College	92,928	661	653	610	760	£1,890,138	£1,768,137	£20.34	£21.52	£2,849	311	292	326
385	Woking College	91,661	668	685	669	681	£1,880,052	£1,956,350	£20.51	£21.92	£2,876	319	308	333
386	Cannington College	90,482	743	759	542	881	£3,176,053	£3,254,153	£35.10	£43.86	£4,725	436	439	420
387	St Mary's College	89,806	676	720	682	682	£2,065,092	£2,180,667	£22.99	£25.02	£3,082	390	386	369
388	Prior Pursglove College	89,786	688	746	669	718	£1,612,206	£1,711,471	£17.95	£19.61	£2,314	169	194	115
389	Hyde-Clarendon College	88,548	773	822	767	767	£2,056,291	£2,164,517	£23.22	£23.79	£2,413	393	365	147
390	Myerscough College	88,537	808	912	666	1,167	£2,767,223	£3,027,596	£31.25	£37.51		431	435	436
391	Berkshire College of Agriculture (The)	87,012	690	649	465	1,148	£1,956,062	£1,737,178	£22.48	£25.12	£3,150	379	387	378
392	Notre Dame Sixth Form College	86,923	654	691	665	665	£1,707,182	£1,770,936	£19.64	£21.35	£2,571	282	281	210

Comparison of Further Education Colleges Ordered Highest 94/95 Funding Units First

06-Sep-94

Count	College	94/95 Funding Units	93/4 Actual Wt FTE	93/94 Wt FTE Target	93/94 Target FTE	93/94 Target Students	94/95 Recurrent Grant	93/94 Recurrent Grant	ALF 94/95	ALF 93/94	Unit Cost 92/93	94/95 ALF Rank	93/94 ALF Rank	92/93 Unit Cost Rank
393	Cleveland College of Art & Design	86,843	763	813	591	779	£2,103,071	£2,234,932	£24.21	£26.70	£3,140	404	401	376
394	Plymouth College of Art & Design	86,840	777	800	574	712	£2,040,686	£2,010,528	£23.49	£26.21	£3,017	394	394	360
395	South Park Sixth Form College	86,502	647	645	589	589	£1,559,650	£1,469,981	£18.03	£18.55	£2,292	179	128	111
396	St Dominic's Sixth Form College	86,410	557	567	533	533	£1,803,994	£1,751,450	£21.37	£22.00	£2,777	352	311	301
397	Askham Bryan College of Agric. & Aylesbury College	84,371	791	772	570	1,398	£2,397,896	£2,383,594	£28.42	£34.09	£3,449	421	427	396
398	Farnham College	83,397	639	619	595	621	£1,775,869	£1,781,213	£21.29	£21.56	£2,789	349	296	310
399	South Bolton Sixth Form College	83,136	605	613	573	573	£1,743,980	£1,649,934	£20.97	£23.38	£2,681	337	353	263
400	Wyggeston Collegiate Sixth Form College	81,874	603	591	576	576	£1,951,066	£1,892,402	£23.83	£24.97	£3,148	398	383	377
401	Eastbourne Sixth Form College	81,449	602	657	624	624	£1,648,380	£1,718,853	£20.23	£22.59	£2,605	305	326	225
402	St Mary's RC College	80,742	615	617	583	583	£1,933,875	£1,843,541	£23.95	£26.59	£3,039	400	399	362
403	Hartlepool Sixth Form College	79,266	583	609	578	578	£1,778,774	£1,831,899	£22.44	£24.17	£3,073	376	370	368
404	Staffordshire College of Agriculture	77,561	785	625	447	638	£1,772,489	£1,741,148	£22.85	£24.96	£2,910	386	382	339
405	Moulton College	77,074	574	491	358	952	£1,755,605	£1,538,655	£22.77	£22.81	£3,262	432	335	386
406	Merrist Wood College	77,024	793	753	538	863	£2,416,561	£2,416,561	£31.37	£33.77	£3,752	386	425	407
407	City of Leeds College of Music	75,729	795	879	630	1,990	£1,645,287	£1,645,287	£21.72	£24.98	£2,286	363	385	108
408	Paston Sixth Form College	75,649	564	603	571	616	£1,481,612	£1,567,843	£19.58	£21.11	£2,567	274	272	209
409	East Norfolk Sixth Form College	73,803	501	518	484	484	£1,339,778	£1,261,561	£18.15	£19.23	£2,406	188	175	142
410	Spelthorne College	72,949	538	585	569	711	£1,523,359	£1,590,145	£20.88	£22.93	£2,744	331	343	290
411	Warwickshire College for Agriculture & Hort.	72,508	656	547	391	874	£1,748,464	£1,559,736	£24.11	£23.27	£3,976	402	350	412
412	Lackham College	71,534	590	572	409	911	£1,783,956	£1,771,555	£24.93	£27.63	£3,795	411	407	409
413	Brooksby College	69,391	509	543	388	812	£1,694,000	£1,680,556	£24.41	£30.91	£3,725	407	418	404
414	Acklam Sixth Form College	68,480	627	637	604	604	£1,644,255	£1,752,937	£24.01	£27.93	£2,799	401	409	315
415	Rutland Sixth Form College	68,116	471	554	524	559	£1,630,013	£1,793,194	£23.93	£28.36	£3,263	399	411	387
416	College of Care & Early Education	67,697	554	538	400	586	£1,133,574	£1,042,846	£16.74	£17.78	£2,393	102	101	440
417	Cumbria College of Art & Design	67,218	566	573	409	409	£1,419,087	£1,406,429	£21.11	£22.55	£2,650	341	324	253
418	Easton College	63,457	752	637	458	1,082	£1,367,357	£1,186,942	£21.54	£23.36	£2,575	360	352	214
419	Hadlow College of Agriculture & Horticulture	60,541	575	627	455	1,082	£2,301,350	£2,531,738	£38.01	£44.11	£4,743	438	440	421
420	Merton Sixth Form College	58,288	371	454	444	444	£1,417,745	£1,527,742	£24.32	£28.99	£2,891	405	413	337

Comparison of Further Education Colleges Ordered Highest 94/95 Funding Units First

06-Sep-94

Count	College	94/95 Funding Units	93/4 Actual Wt FTE	93/94 Wt FTE Target	93/94 Target FTE	93/94 Target Students	94/95 Recurrent Grant	93/94 Recurrent Grant	ALF 94/95	ALF 93/94	Unit Cost 92/93	94/95 ALF Rank	93/94 ALF Rank	92/93 Units Cost Rank
421	Berkshire College of Art & Design	56,614	517	552	395	772	£1,716,028	£1,863,223	£30.31	£33.71	£3,994	427	424	413
422	Brackenhurst College	56,384	439	423	327	691	£1,730,464	£1,740,909	£30.69	£35.41	£4,554	428	431	417
423	De La Salle College	55,155	445	528	512	512	£1,354,920	£1,490,561	£24.56	£29.31	£2,870	410	414	331
424	Bede College	54,400	349	434	394	394	£1,140,870	£1,147,757	£20.97	£26.31	£2,684	336	396	265
425	Herefordshire College of Art & Design	52,430	433	473	338	412	£989,612	£1,024,443	£18.87	£21.79	£2,527	243	301	193
426	Epsom School of Art & Design	51,972	425	498	356	356	£1,528,172	£1,662,864	£29.40	£35.30	£3,686	426	430	403
427	Norfolk Institute of Art & Design	51,236	400	405	289	289	£1,251,786	£1,167,711	£24.43	£28.80	£3,185	408	412	380
428	Writtle Agricultural College	50,257	508	511	365	758	£1,807,443	£1,807,443	£35.96	£42.32	£3,743	437	438	405
429	Plumpton College	48,197	535	471	337	1,000	£1,308,093	£1,317,314	£27.14	£32.10	£3,096	417	422	370
430	Broomfield College	47,029	542	389	278	695	£1,528,260	£1,528,260	£32.49	£36.06	£4,025	434	433	414
431	Cambridgeshire College of Agriculture	40,531	307	363	266	601	£1,262,967	£1,386,352	£31.16	£39.02	£4,351	430	436	415
432	Rycotewood College	39,349	295	294	210	245	£1,153,915	£1,148,174	£29.32	£33.80	£4,618	425	426	418
433	Pershore College of Horticulture	37,574	374	383	273	437	£1,446,351	£1,492,622	£38.49	£47.78	£4,746	439	441	422
434	Walford (Agricultural) College, Shropshire	37,358	379	402	287	669	£1,190,824	£1,301,447	£31.87	£36.53	£3,527	433	434	398
435	Durham College of Horticulture & Agriculture	34,694	357	348	248	564	£1,140,767	£1,140,767	£32.88	£35.16	£3,904	435	429	411
436	Marton Sixth Form College	33,965	306	298	282	282	£1,058,364	£1,114,067	£31.16	£31.16	£3,840	429	435	410
437	Capel Manor Horticultural & Environmental College	33,926	344	284	208	721	£1,314,221	£1,314,221	£38.73	£34.71	£4,422	440	420	416
438	Kirkley Hall College	25,728	368	277	203	526	£1,088,023	£1,088,023	£42.28	£39.62	£5,579	441	437	423
439	Northern School of Contemporary Dance	22,240	148	150	107	107	£331,043	£326,472	£14.88	£15.20	£3,198	27	23	381
440	Herefordshire College of Agriculture	20,667	195	233	166	317	£569,613	£620,493	£27.56	£35.96	£3,744	419	432	406
441	Worcestershire College of Agriculture	15,556	139	168	120	558	£427,733	£409,706	£27.49	£29.66	£3,515	418	416	397
442	Kingston Maurward College	0		766	551	1,649	£0	£0	£999.00	£999.00	£1,667	443	444	5
443	Stockport College of Further & Higher Education	0		4,910	3,999	11,993	£0	£0	£999.00	£999.00	£3,356	442	443	392
444	South Kent College	0		3,668	3,126	7,144	£0	£0	£999.00	£999.00	£1,957	444	442	27
445	Dewsbury College	0		2,881	2,452	7,064	£0	£0	£999.00	£999.00	£2,805	445	447	318
446	Aylesbury College	0		2,823	2,375	6,609	£0	£0	£999.00	£999.00	£2,087	446	446	50
447	Exeter College	0		4,318	3,879	8,729	£0	£0	£999.00	£999.00	£2,149	447	445	63

Exercises

EXERCISE 1: Strategic and Operational Planning
  1 Know your college: Facts and figures
  2 Investigate financial risk
  3 Determine SWOT analysis summary
  4 Produce action plan: Opportunities, weaknesses, threats
  5 Determining strategic objectives
  6 Establishing measurable goals
  7 Determining estates objectives

EXERCISE 2: Financial Planning, Management and Control
  1 Preparing for the exercise
  2 Listing key assumptions as a base for financial forecasts
  3 Considering the coverage of the financial forecasts
  4 Defining the information requirements for financial planning
  5 Describing the system for staff planning, monitoring and control
  6 Listing the main features of your college's equipment replacement policy
  7 Describing the treatment of depreciation
  8 Checking the adequacy of your college's cash flow systems
  9 Defining the messages of the year end accounts

EXERCISE 3: Business Functions and Services
  1 Calculating the cost of contracted in business services
  2 Effectiveness of purchasing procedures
  3 Payroll management
  4 Adequacy of treasury policy
  5 Examining the college's estates strategy
  6 Audit needs assessment and audit plan

EXERCISE 4: Income and Expenditure
  1 Establishing trends in income
  2 Establishing trends in expenditure
  3 Investigate income/expenditure variances

4 Analyze recurrent funding allocation by entry/ on programme/ achievement
5 Analyze recurrent funding allocation by academic departments
6 Analysis of the sensitivity of income and expenditure levels to change
7 Checking the adequacy of your college's fees policy

EXERCISE 5: **Internal Resourcing, Unit Costing, Budgeting**
1 Locating income to departments
2 Locating expenditure to departments
3 Determining staffing expenditure
4 Producing a 'service level agreement'

EXERCISE 6: **Performance Measurement and Monitoring**
1 Understand monitoring responsibilities
2 Setting targets
3 Determining information requirements for monitoring
4 Taking corrective action
5 Deciding which performance indicators to use
6 Establishing FEFC performance indicators trends
7 Recording transactions
8 Implementation of the individual student record

EXERCISE 7: **Improving Efficiency and Increasing Income**
1 Improving efficiency
2 Examining earned income by client company
3 Increasing earned income

EXERCISE 8: **Inter-College Comparisons**
1 Determining how your college ranks against other colleges. Use graphs and charts
2 Comparing your college with other similar colleges

Bibliography and Further Reading

The Further Education Funding Council has produced many useful publications including the following:

1 *Guide for College Governors* — The Further Education Funding Council
2 FEFC Circular 93/39: *Recurrent Funding for 1994–95*
3 FEFC Circular 94/10: *ISR Data Collection 1994–95*
4 FEFC Circular 94/23: *Modified Audit Evidence for Entry Units 1994–95*
5 FEFC Circular 94/30: *College Strategic Plans*
6 FEFC Circular 94/31: *Measuring Achievement*

Further Reading

1 FEFC Guides on the complex subject of Charitable Status

2 Use of subsidiary companies
   - Converting profit from subsidiaries
   - Companies Act account procedures
   - Role and responsibilities of directors of subsidiary companies
   - Consolidated accounts

3 VAT
   - Group VAT registration to maximize colleges VAT position, given the generally poor ratio of inputs:outputs
   - Energy purchase through subsidiary to mitigate VAT charges

4 Governors' responsibilities
   - Cadbury Report
   - Public Accounts Committee
   - Use of policy and procedure documentation (an increasingly important safeguard for governors)

5   Comparators
    The FEFC has produced some useful base comparators for all
    groups of colleges, for example
            % staffing salary
            % estates costs
            % depreciation
            % debtor/creditor days
    Reference to these would be useful